THE GROWTH MERCHANTS

Economic Consequences
of Wishful Thinking

THE GROWTH MERCHANTS

Economic Consequences of
Wishful Thinking

ROBIN PRINGLE

 Centre for Policy Studies   London 1977

Centre for Policy Studies
London 1976.

First published 1977
by Centre for Policy Studies
Wilfred Street
London S.W.1.
Typeset and Printed by
The Pentagon Printing Group,
Soho Square, London W1V 5TW.
ISBN 0 9504392 4 X
© Robin Pringle

Contents

Foreword

by Rt. Hon. Sir Keith Joseph MP

BEHIND the many causes of our disappointing economic performance over the last 30 years has lain a continuing disagreement about the management of the economy. Until recently the fashionable orthodoxy — based on the misapplication of Keynes' teaching — has been to ignore the significance of the relationship between the growth in monetary aggregates and the growth in the supply of goods and services. To-day that orthodoxy is under challenge, but it is still necessary to examine why politicians did not long ago recognise the damage that our policies were doing to the country, especially in comparison with the different policies and better performance of a number of our neighbours.

Of course the politicians must take the blame. Their words and predictions are rightly held against them when they prove wrong. Academics and journalists are quick to find politicians at fault.

But are the journalists and those academics, who take on the role of advising governments, as guitless as they imagine themselves to be? Should not their analyses and predictions be monitored also?

Robin Pringle is a journalist who has, over the past decade and more, been associated with one of the more consistent voices of dissent. *The Banker*, of which he is the distinguished editor, has habitually emphasised the overriding importance of monetary rectitude.

In this booklet he analyses the theme-music of those who have — with the honourable and disregarded exception of his own publication — helped to provide the orchestration to the public discussion of economic management in Britain during the past two decades: the Bank of England *Quarterly,* the *Review* of the National Institute of Economic and Social Research, *The Economist* newspaper; and not forgetting the contribution of those who, like Mr Andrew Shonfield, and Mr Christopher Dow, have straddled the borderlines between *academe,* journalism, and the civil service.

The relationship between the journalists on the one hand and the politicians and civil servants on the other is always an ambivalent one. Politicians need a good press: yet they are generally mistrustful of journalists. All the evidence over the years suggests that the popular press has little or no influence in shaping the opinions of the mass electorate (although it can strengthen its prejudices): yet politicians regularly behave as if editorial opinions in the mass-circulation newspapers both shaped and reflected electoral attitudes. Relatively few politicians, by contrast, worry their heads over the opinions expressed in the journals which are the subject of this critique: they reflect that *their* electors have never heard of the Bank of England *Quarterly,* and rarely read *The Economist.*

By contrast the influence of these publications in Whitehall is very considerable. It is not only that the senior civil servants are themselves their avid readers, and bask in their approval — or shrink at their disapprobation, as the case may be — for the strategies they have helped to devise. It is also that they know that the views of these publications are widely studied and quoted overseas. (The attitudes of respect is reciprocated: it was no freak of editorial fancy which made it virtually impossible for advocates of devaluation to secure a hearing in the mid-1960s. Editors knew that the mere publication of articles on this unmentionable subject in authoritative journals could become self-fulfilling).

Thus the consistently "expansionist" bias given to its forecasts by the National Institute, which underestimate the pressure on domestic resources, and the growth of imports, while overestimating the growth of exports, has powerfully reinforced the dominance of neo-Keynesian attitudes at the Treasury and the CBI, and eventually, by the end of the 1960s, had begun to shame the Bank of England out of its natural caution. The expansionist clamour reached its climax in 1972-73, when the warnings of *The Banker,* some individuals and groups in the City and in academic life and some on the Government's back benches in the House of Commons were swamped by the chorus of approval for the official strategy of "five *per cent* growth"; and those within the Administration who experienced occasional qualms found reassurance in the ebullient enthusiasm — so devastatingly chronicled by Robin Pringle in this survey — of *The Economist.*

The wisdom of hindsight is the privilege of journalism. No one coming fresh to the verdict of National Institute and *Economist* on the collapse of the boom in 1974 could guess that these same voices had been cheering on the headlong monetary expansion of 1972. When challenged, they had their alibi: the unforeseen escalation of world commodity prices. Yet, as Mr Pringle reminds us, it was also these voices which had been the first to denounce overseas governments — most notably that of Western Germany — which *had* foreseen the coming storm and taken early action to shorten sail, for selfish irresponsibility.

This does not exonerate the politicians from the lion's share of responsibility for our present predicament. All inflations down the ages have been caused by governments, which alone can halt them. Indeed Mr Pringle is, if anything, too kind to the politicians: thus, he blames the Bank of England for its distaste for the use of interest rate policy to control the money supply, although this is a distaste at least equally shared by the politicians (albeit for different reasons).

Nevertheless the politicians *have* been aided and abetted in their errors, and not by the civil servants alone. It takes unusual determination to resist the insidious tide of editorials forever calling for state-sponsored expansionism and the administrative control of incomes — particularly when such activism, though repeatedly tried and found wanting, accords with the politician's natural desire to justify his own existence. In another respect also, as Mr Pringle reminds us, the limitations of journalism and politics have been mutually reinforcing. Both have short time-scales, and their practitioners think instinctively in terms of "action this day". Mr Pringle draws our attention to the symptomatic justification by Chancellor Healey of his rejection of public expenditure restraint in the summer of 1975: that it could not possibly be effective "even on the theory held by the monetarists" in time. Recognition of the inevitably long time-lags between action and reaction in economic management flies in the face of political instincts, so what hope is there when those same instincts are reinforced by the lust for manipulation of the neo-Keynesians on the sidelines?

Perhaps the answer to this question is "more than there has been these twenty years past". Perhaps this is the darkness before dawn. "Growth" has almost passed from public debate. It is more widely understood now that growth is not properly an objective so much as a by-product of rational policies. Some of the most influential economic writers — Samuel Brittan, Peter Jay, Patrick Hutber — now consistently denounce the repetition of past follies. Even *The Economist* approves the setting of specific money supply targets. Before many months are out one more experiment with incomes control will have collapsed, and already the Chancellor and his officials are reporting once a quarter to the probationary officers of the International Monetary Fund. Perhaps the foundations of a return to a healthier British economy have been laid.

But there will still be dangers. It is all too easy as we saw in 1972-73 — when I was in part responsible — to be carried away by short-term pressures that will, if general economic policies be correct, solve themselves. Should we make that sort of mistake again, then nothing will save us from full-blown currency collapse.

Mr Pringle's is, therefore, a text for our time: a reminder of past events which ought to ensure that if the siren voices he chronicles are raised again, they are for once ignored.

Ken Joseph.

1. The Treason of the Economic Establishment

THIS study was written at a time when the economy was making a half-hearted recovery from a deep recession. The Government appeared in 1976 to have abandoned post-war neo-Keynesian economic policies, in that official policy was not directed primarily to restoring full employment in the short term, but rather to regaining internal and external equilibrium and particularly to curbing further the rate of price inflation which was still running at about 15 *per cent.* Leading newspapers were publishing articles proclaiming the end of the Keynesian era. The monetarist view, according to which governments do not have it in their power to regulate employment in the long term, was in the ascendant. Future macro-economic policy, according to this view, should confine itself to following clear rules, such as holding down the growth of the money supply to a rate not exceeding the expected rate of growth of productive capacity.

The full monetarist position had not been accepted, however, by the government or by more than a minority of academic economists. It was still hard to expect any democratically elected government to be prepared to declare itself impotent in the matter of securing full employment by measures of overall "demand management". Instead, the UK Government, like others, found themselves in 1975-76 forced to adopt what may be termed "*ad hoc* monetarism" — a spell of monetary restraint, along with concomitant high levels of unemployment (by post-war standards) whilst inflation was reduced. *Ad hoc* monetarism is as old as the hills. It is a convenient shorthand for the policies followed by every British Chancellor who has had the bad luck to hold that office during one of the "stop" phases of the go-stop cycle.

There can be no remedy for inflation and the steadily rising prices which go with it which does not include, and indeed is not founded upon, a control of the money supply.

Thus Mr Thorneycroft (now Lord Thorneycroft) as Chancellor in 1957. In 1962 Mr Selwyn Lloyd (now Lord Selwyn-Lloyd) brought in a tough budget when the economy had already been stagnant for two years and was accused of having abandoned Keynesian economics. Mr Roy Jenkins devoted much of his time as Chancellor in 1967-70 to attaining monetary targets set in negotiation with the International Monetary Fund. Mr Healey began to tread the same path in 1975-76. None of these Chancellors or their advisers accepted "monetarism" as an academic doctrine. After their restrictive policies had covered the government's exposed flanks, there was nothing to stop *ad hoc* monetarism from giving way to renewed expansion.

To be sure there has, in recent years, been a clear change in opinion towards a greater degree of attention to monetary influences. But the extent of the change should not be exaggerated. At the time, the measures taken by previous governments were written up in the press not just as *ad hoc* responses to economic difficulties but as policies with a definite rationale. There is a cycle in economic comment as well as in the economy itself; during one of the expansionary phases it is difficult to recollect the mood that prevailed in the restrictive phase, and vice versa.

Successive rounds of this go-stop cycle have, however, taken place at higher rates of both unemployment and inflation. The 1972-75 cycle gave Britain its first whiff of hyper-inflation. Presumably, the choice is therefore stark: either policy dismounts from the merry-go-round which it has ridden for 30 years, or inflation and unemployment will eventually reach such levels simultaneously as to spark an explosion after which the economy will collapse in on itself in the social equivalent of the astronomers' "black hole".

It does rather matter which of these possibilities comes to pass. To pose the choice, in however stark a manner, does not in itself help to ensure the preferred outcome. Dire warnings have been delivered before. There are many remedies on offer besides the prescriptions of monetarism. The worse the outlook, the more fertile the ground for quack remedies, such as import controls; for illusions, such as dreams of salvation from North

Sea oil; and for continued argument – many Argentinian economists remain convinced that their country's 200 *per cent* inflation is still the result wholly of "cost-push" and not of an excessive growth in the money supply.

Facts and warnings cannot resolve such arguments: many observers have tried to expose the dangers inherent in acceptance of neo-Keynesianism for many years. If they have failed, by economic arguments, to convert the economic establishment, what can succeed? The following pages suggest that an understanding of the social environment in which policy is formulated, and persistent questioning of conventional assumptions, might free policy from the grip of the pressures in which it is trapped. Why has Britain not got off the roundabout before? Why wait until it has reduced the economy to such a weak state? How did this happen to us?

Such are the questions with which this pamphlet deals. It does not seek to expose "guilty men", but rather the guilty, or at least mistaken, polices. This pamphlet argues that the polices followed in fact were the products of a number of inconsistent economic ideas and of unfortunate advice tendered by the particular institutions involved in economic policy. The dominant ideology was neo-Keynesianism (an ideology derived from the writings of John Maynard Keynes of King's College, Cambridge); the institutions were the Treasury, the Bank of England, the press and members of the Cambridge University economics faculty. Together they created a distinctive climate of opinion which gave birth to mis-shapen policies.

It is as important to explore the reasons why policy has taken this shape as it is to understand the academic debate between "Keynesians" and "monetarists". (Indeed, a tendency to exaggerate the differences between these two schools of economic thought has perhaps obscured some of the crucial policy dilemmas faced by governments). To focus on theoretical questions may not be the best way of changing the course of policy (especially as monetarism in its modern dress arrived in Britain from Chicago firmly, if unfairly, labelled with a right-wing political ticket).

Even if monetarism as such were not to become official economic doctrine, many of its basic tenets could be adopted,

3

or re-adopted, as guides to policy. The notions that a government's expenditure should be kept in some reasonable relationship to the revenue it can raise by non-punitive rates of taxation and that a rapid depreciation of the currency is to be avoided at all costs have been accepted by governments of many political complexions for many hundreds of years — and even followed by some of them. They have been followed more faithfully in England than anywhere else, and England has accordingly had a stable currency and political tradition over a longer period than any other comparable country. What has to be explained is how, halfway through the twentieth century, such a comparatively stable country started to adopt such an extraordinarily inflationary economic policy.

The answer is not simply "Keynesian economics" nor is it simply "the trades unions". The ways in which these ideas and institutions, along with others, came to influence policy, and the channels through which this influence was exerted, are problems to be investigated, not things to be taken for granted. In the language of sociology, the question is how economic policies come to be accepted as "legitimate"; what factors set the boundaries of "political acceptability" within which economic policy options are debated by practical men; and how the economic policies actually adopted may contain glaring inconsistencies that economists of any school can recognize as likely to render that policy unsustainable or harmful.

This analysis is therefore addressed as much to "neo-Keynesians" as to "monetarists" or those attracted to alternative analyses such as the "new Cambridge" school or the presentation by Bacon and Eltis (see *Britain's Economic Problem: Too Few Producers,* Robert Bacon and Walter Eltis, [Macmillan Press, 1976]). It deliberately tries to avoid taking sides in such debates, though it does ask Keynesians to recognize that theirs has been the dominant ideology in post-war policy. Rather it looks at the institutions which actually make policy or influence it and the ideas they have held. Readers are invited to consider the structure of the argument as a whole rather than particular points of economic controversy within it and, even if they disagree, to "suspend disbelief" for a time, as if they were at a play.

4

Behind Stop-Go

In the view of impartial observers the UK economy has
repeatedly overshot the mark in the "go" phases of its post-war
business (and electoral) cycles, leading to unnecessarily harsh
"stops", with damaging effects on confidence, investment and
growth prospects. In the words of one "authoritative" external
observer:

> The United Kingdom has had a succession of periods when demand
> was allowed — or, indeed, was encouraged by policy measures — to
> grow at a rate which, in the event, appeared excessive; followed by
> periods when restrictive action had to be taken.
>
> Budget action has . . . tended to reinforce short-term
> fluctuations of output and employment rather than correct them.
> In fact, during the 1960s demand management appears, by and
> large, to have served to create such fluctuations. The period 1955-57
> provides an exception to this generalization when because of its
> automatic effects, the budget helped to stabilize the economy.
> Otherwise, upswings have been strongly accelerated by discretionary
> budget policy and other policy instruments, to the point at which
> the balance of payments turned into deficit and speculative capital
> outflows began. This happened in 1954-55 and was repeated in
> 1959-60 and 1963-64. In each case policy had to be reversed, with
> increasing unemployment and slow-down of the growth rate as a
> result of the well-known "stop-go" cycle. The basic error leading to
> this cycle has lain in allowing demand to expand too fast to an
> undesirably high level.

The OECD report from which these extracts are taken, *Fiscal
Policy for a Balanced Economy,* appeared in 1968; its account
and explanation remain as valid today. Its 1975 report on the
UK economy, though showing signs of more than usually close
vetting by the British government, described the latest go-stop
in these flat sentences:

> At the beginning of 1973 the Government was aiming for rapid
> growth of output over the short and medium-term. Policy was
> stimulatory, sterling had been allowed to float downwards to
> encourage exports and import substitution and statutory prices and
> incomes controls were moving towards the second of what
> became a three-stage programme. Although the rate of growth of
> demand and activity slowed down considerably through 1973, the
> prospect of excess demand in 1974 promoted restrictive demand

management measures towards the end of the year. At the same time the rate of inflation increased and the current balance of payments position deteriorated markedly largely reflecting the steep rise in commodity prices and strong domestic demand pressure.

A longer-range international study — that by the Brookings Institution — gave a similar judgement. Overall fiscal policy effects were "generally perverse" for the price level and the balance of payments; and tax changes were such as to be "perversely related to current growth rates", thus "tending to emphasize the growth cycles". *(Britain's Economic Prospects,* Richard Caves and associates of the Brooking's Institution, [George Allen and Unwin, 1968]). Or, as Professor Beckerman wearily remarked,

> The manner in which investment in Britain has been affected by "stop-go" policies is too familiar to require much elaboration. (*The British Economy in 1975,* W. Beckerman and Associates, [Cambridge University Press, 1965], p.51).

Mr Christopher Dow, who is now at the Bank of England, after another exhaustive 444-page study, arrived at an equally unequivocal verdict:

> As far as internal conditions are concerned, then, budget and monetary policy failed to be stabilizing, and must on the contrary be regarded as having been positively destabilizing (J.C.R. Dow, *The Management of the British Economy 1945-60,* [Cambridge University Press, 1967], p.384).

Since these books were published another boom (1972-73) has been followed by the worst ever post-war slump, both occurring at unprecedently high rates of inflation.

The important thing to remember in considering such evidence is that one does not have to take sides in the monetarist *v* Keynesian controversy to be impressed by it. It has nothing to do with such debates. On *any* view, "growth" policies led to "stops", unnecessarily accentuating the normal business cycle; more importantly, over successive cycles the balance of the economy has been shifted towards consumption and public spending — these being the two ways in which demand has been stimulated — and away from exports and investment. It is the shape of the go-stop cycle as much as the cycle itself that has distorted the UK economy.

6

Why so De-stabilizing?

The authorities cited, and others which could be added to them, offered various reasons for the erratic and perverse course of official economic policy:

1. *Optimistic forecasts.* These were stressed by the OECD study: "Excessive optimism concerning the scope for expansion was certainly a factor underlying the unfortunate developments of 1964-65" (p.66); the "undesirably expansionary" policies in both 1959 and 1963-64 appear to have been partly due to an underestimation of the buoyancy of demand, or an overestimation of the room for expansion". Significantly, on the rare occasions when policy appeared too restrictive, optimism was still partly to blame: "excessively optimistic export forecasts . . . may have been one factor leading the British Government to abstain from expansionary budget measures in 1962": and, it may be added, on occasion since. Equally, optimistic forecasts of investment have often been made (since the Treasury started publishing regular economic forecasts at Budget time, it has forecast a rise in investment on average nearly twice as large as was in fact achieved). The trouble is partly due to repeated over-estimation of the amount of "growth" the economy could achieve without "overheating", and partly a tendency in both "stop" and "go" phases of the cycle to hold optimistic views about the strength of "good" components of final demand, like exports and investment: this characteristic of the forecasts suggests a more general climate of wishful thinking. The public expenditure plans as outlined in recent White Papers, which have come to be seen as over-ambitious, often as soon as they were off the presses, provide further illustrations of this tendency.

2. *Optimism on the underlying growth of capacity.* In the "Neddy" phase of the early 1960s, 4 *per cent* was set as a realistic objective for the annual underlying growth of capacity and thus of output (with a 3.2 *per cent* annual rise in output per man). Demand was stimulated by official policy to grow accordingly. This 4 *per cent* rate was, as Neddy recognised, "a much faster rate of increase than was experienced on average during the last 10 years" (National Economic Development Council, *The Growth of the Economy,* March 1964, p.22).

7

However, this warning about the ambitious nature of the 4 *per cent* figure served only to preface paragraphs dealing with what Neddy regarded as equally important subjects such as whether the sand and gravel industry could cope with the anticipated upsurge in demand. Confidently, Neddy asserted that "the check to productivity growth in 1960 reflected in part supply limitations, but such limitations may be less operative in 1964". In the event, the year 1964 (the Neddy report appeared as late as March) was a year during which there was severe overheating, as virtually everybody later conceded. Neddy might have done a service by stressing more openly the leap in productivity that its macro-economists assumed was possible: for in the years 1948-60 national output had grown on average by only 2.75 *per cent* a year and output per man by a bare 2 *per cent*. But Mr Selwyn Lloyd had not established Neddy as an agency for spreading realism but as a little temple to growth.

Similarly in 1973-75: in 1973 the underlying growth in productivity was put at about 3 − 3.5 *per cent* by the National Institute, on the assumption that it had been on a secularly rising trend since 1960. This estimate underlay the Institute's assumption of a 5 *per cent* gap between actual and potential output at the end of 1972, and thus behind its recommendation of a neutral budget in 1973 at a time when total demand, spurred by previous fiscal and monetary stimuli, was expected to increase at an annual rate of 5 *per cent*. Plainly, as it insisted then, on these assumptions there was "no imminent resource clash" (National Institute Economic Review, February 1973, p.6). In other words, 5 *per cent* per annum growth for a period was feasible. By 1975 the picture presented by NIESR itself was, however, very different:

> ... the 1973 experience of a growth rate of GDP of more than 5 *per cent*, accompanied by an increase in productivity of only 2.5 *per cent*, looks particularly poor ... It is not now possible to assume an underlying productivity trend of more than 2.5 − 3 *per cent* per annum ... (NIESR, February 1975).

So much for their earlier forecast. But what damage had been done to price stability and the balance of payments in the meantime by the expansionary policies it had encouraged the Government to take? When NIESR's mistakes become too glaring even for its own comfort, it tries to rescue its claim to be "scientific" by analysing them after the event; like other institutions, it appears, however, incapable of preventing them from recurring.

In this case, the over-estimate of the underlying uptrend in output per man and in the margin of spare capacity meant that unemployment fell in 1973 much faster than the Institute had expected and there were clear signs of strain in the labour market in the second half of the year, though the Institute later insisted that this was a "regional problem". This was also Mr Heath's view. Moreover, this overheating occurred despite the unforecast plunge into deficit in the balance of payments (which the Institute — and the Treasury — had typically assumed would improve when in fact it was plunging into the red to an unprecendented extent). This unexpectedly *drained* spending power out of the economy — and indeed occurred, on one interpretation, partly at least *because* of the existence of excess demand. The deficit and the rise in import prices associated with it cut real disposable incomes by about 3 *per cent.* Pressure on capacity would have been all the greater if this unexpected development had not taken place. So, although the instrument of deflation was on this occasion partly external, the *need* for corrective action was just as great as in previous "stop-go" cycles and was created in a similar way — by optimistic assumptions of the degree of slack and of the rate of productivity growth leading to over-rapid expansion.

3. *Concentration on the short-term prospects.* The occasions on which this habit has tripped up forecasts and policy are too numerous to recite: in particular, the length of the time lags between policy measures and their results is invariably under-estimated. Suffice to quote Mr Dow again:

> It is difficult not to feel that too little weight was given to . . .
> secondary and delayed effects of policy changes; and that the long
> train of repercussions out of which, over years, a boom builds up,
> was not reckoned with. For this neglect . . . the practice of making
> annual forecasts of developments to be expected in the year ahead
> was partly responsible. For short-run forecasting may often be done
> by what amounts to short cuts — which fail to focus attention on
> basic causal sequences (op, cit. p.392).

This verdict on forecasting remains as valid as when it was

written. The error is personified by those politicians who ask: "well, what would *you* have done in November 1973, when the oil-price rise hit us?" or, "what would *you* have done in June 1975, when sterling came under such pressure and inflation was riding about 30 *per cent*?" The answer could be to run the economy on completely different lines.

4. *Undue reliance on conventional indicators.* The economic indicator which forecasters have used in Britain hitherto to estimate the room for expansion has essentially been the unemployment rate, with some reference to the level of unfilled vacancies, the Bank of England's index of capacity utilization in manufacturing, and the CBI index based on its regular surveys of industrial trends. Research has suggested that these are all seriously deficient, for a wide variety of reasons. The weakness of the unemployment ratio, as conventionally defined, have been spelled out by Samuel Brittan in *Second Thoughts on Full Employment Policy* (Barry Rose for CPS, 1975). Jim Taylor and Stuart McKendrick, in a survey of these indicators, found them all to be mis-leading: "the pressure of demand over the last decade has been severely under-estimated by the conventional indicators, with the exception of the CBI index" *(Lloyds Bank Review,* January 1975, p.25). In my view even more important, however, is the *bias* that is given to policy recommendations whatever the indicator from which they are derived: this is what this pamphlet seeks to prove.

5. *The belief that excess demand does not matter very much.* The reviews of the NIESR in particular have encouraged this belief. On one occasion in 1973 it asserted that when economic growth slows down because capacity is fully utilised, demand will happily decline of its own accord:

> When supply constraints inhibit output, they usually inhibit at the same time the incomes which that output would have generated; consequently the secondary effects, incorporated in any demand-type model, will also fail to occur. Thus without any action by the authorities the deceleration of output will in many cases be accompanied by a deceleration of demand — though not necessarily to the same extent.

Such statements may be interpreted as virtually ruling out the danger of demand inflation, thus throwing most economic literature on the subject out of the window: quite a permissible exercise, but surely the Institute should have warned readers what it was doing.

6. *Silence over the exchange rate.* Most economic forecasts and plans for faster growth were silent on the subject of the sterling exchange rate up to 1967. Neddy, the NIESR and the large volumes of research quoted above kept it well in the background. When, most inconsiderately, the balance of payments nevertheless plunged into the red, they muttered about the need to improve competitiveness and smartly changed the subject. Long chapters were, instead, devoted to ways and means of improving the *supply* of goods and services, leading to talk about planning, the educational system, the class system, the shortage of engineers and do on. Thus the taboo surrounding the exchange rate issue helped in a roundabout way to raise further the illusory hopes held for physical planning and other non-market ways of tackling the problem of Britain's growing uncompetitiveness.

7. *The promise of growth.* There is, however, another background reason for the repetition of so many of the mistakes from one cycle to another: the belief that low growth has been due to the single cause of too great caution and restraint in demand policy. A Prime Minister hearing this, whether Mr Macmillan in 1962 or Mr Heath in 1972, will prick up his ears. Because one thing that governments can promise as their part of a strategy to get the economy moving, is to keep monetary demand expanding. They can print the stuff.

This obsession with growth may well have been a principal reason preventing growth from being achieved. The way it came to dominate policy deserves a chapter in itself; because it was this obsession that converted the relatively innocuous "stop-go" policy cycle of the 1950s and 1960s into the highly inflationary policies of the 1970s. The seeds of this transformation had been sown, however, many years previously.

2. *The Growth Bug*

THE most powerful single notion of post-war economics has been that the aim of full employment can and should be attained by expansionary budgetary policies. This was the message that Lord Keynes had successfully drummed into the Establishment, and into the universities, to such a degree that in Oxbridge only growth-minded "Keynesians" could hope to attain professorial appointments (though mercifully this is less true now of Oxford).

The next most powerful notion is that the rate of long-term growth of the economy can be raised by Keynesian policies too. Keynes himself always seems to have been fairly clear that long-term growth rates were determined by the thrift and enterprise of the people and never suggested that they could be furthered by monetary means; but once his doctrines had led people to instal levers for manipulating demand, it was a natural step to imagine that the same levers could be pulled to make the economy grow too.

The aim of attaining full employment seemed to have been achieved during the 1950s and the definition of "full-employment" was made increasingly ambitious, except when the fixed parity of the pound appeared to stand in the way. It was assumed that this had been made possible by Keynesian full employment policies. The possibility that these worked because of other factors — a world-wide trade boom, a general desire by workers to hold down their jobs after the unemployment of the 1930s, ample investment opportunities opened up by technological progress, reasonably modest expectations of real increases in living standards, reasonable levels of public expenditure and the widespread assumption of reasonably stable prices — was not investigated. Nor was the possibility that pursuit of ever-fuller employment might gradually undermine the conditions necessary for the success of such policies.

The interest of "progressive" thinkers was concentrated increasingly on the apparent obstacles to growth. Gradually, even the old-fashioned attachment to price stability itself came to be regarded as such an obstacle. Andrew Shonfield's book, *British Economic Policy since the War,* published first in 1958, was a milestone on that road:

> The era of Conservative expansion, which was started by Mr R.A. Butler back in 1953, had now (1957) come to an end. Its final death blow was celebrated amidst a chorus of frenzied middle class voices shouting that no sacrifice of real wealth was too great so long as the price tags on goods in the shops could be kept the same.

It became axiomatic for a "progressive" thinker, that only the most reactionary Tories like those few ministers in 1957, led by Peter Thorneycroft, who had to resign as a result, could put price stability first. "The new deflation", continued Mr Shonfield bitterly,

> was motivated neither by the needs of the balance of payments nor by the purpose of relieving a strain on the productive resources of the economy; in 1957 these resources were plainly under-employed. The objective this time was social rather than economic: *stability was an end in itself . . .* (author's italics)

The bulk of the book was devoted to thinking up ways of solving the problems that appeared to be holding up expansion — and in fact it sketched out most of the policies that were to be tried, unsuccessfully, in the following decade: planning, incomes policies, balance-of-payments policies. The aim throughout was to break bottlenecks so that demand — hopefully investment demand — could expand freely. After noting the problems that would ensue, Mr Shonfield observed: "Here are the makings of the familiar crisis of a country trying to get ahead 'too fast':

> *The problem is to ensure that this country will be able to continue to move forward for a few years at this excessive speed, regardless".* (p.280, Penguin Revised Edition [author's italics]).

This general trend of opinion was reflected in countless articles at the time, when Britain had just embarked on three years of stagnation (1960-62), years that seemed to prove the progressive thinkers right in everything they had said.

So the ground was prepared for another boom, Mr Maudling's followed by a plan — Mr Brown's — and one year later the collapse of that plan. But "progressive" thought did not change very much. The new strand, added to the others, was the stress put on an implied need to devalue, to allow expansion to continue. This was, however, rarely stated openly. Readers were usually left to draw their own conclusion. An exception was the writing of Samuel Brittan at that time, whose *Inquest on Planning in Britian,* (Political and Economic Planning; January 1967) amounted to a plea for a liberal, expansionist policy incorporating a flexible exchange rate. The National Plan's experiment in attempting to raise real growth rates by raising demand expectations could have worked, Mr Brittan's message was, if it had not been for the lack of any balance of payments strategy. Calculations that the economy could only grow at 2.5 *per cent* instead of NEDC's 4 *per cent* target were, he said, unduly pessimistic because backward-looking — being based on calculations about how output behaved when it was 'constantly' being held back for balance-of-payments reasons.

The ideology of expansion, now called 'growth', attained through the expansion of monetary demands survived intact. Indeed, it was strengthened, because during the ill-fated National Plan efforts had been made to improve the *supply* of goods by direct action to remove bottlenecks (indicative planning and the rest). As it had failed, there seemed to be nothing left to try except an all-out effort to raise demand, and to hell with the balance of payments (and, by implication, price stability too).

Gradually, the NIESR began to bias its recommended policy measures in favour of maximum expansion. Its *forecasts* had long been biased in a direction that encouraged such policies, as George Polanyi, in a predictably ignored paper (IEA Background Memorandum 4) has demonstrated. (See also *Forecasting the UK Economy,* J.C.K. Ash and D.J. Smyth, Saxon House Studies, 1974). In 1959 output was forecast by NIESR to rise by only 1 *per cent;* it increased by 6.6 *per cent.* In 1963 the forecast was 3.7 *per cent;* the recorded increase was

7.1 *per cent*. True, these forecasts need to be adjusted to take into account the effect of policy actions taken after the forecasts were made; but on the NIESR's own figuring, the errors were still very large — occuring precisely in crucial "boom" years. The balance of payments forecasts had usually been similarly optimistic. The purpose of dwelling on NIESR's forecasts is not to poke fun at them. It is twofold: first, to suggest that forecasting the 'real' economy is such an inexact science that it would be better to base policy on other rules, or use other guidelines, if alternatives are available (and monetarism makes such an alternative rule available); secondly, to suggest that NIESR's forecasts have been biased in such a way as to lead to a persistent under-estimation of the inflationary forces in the economy. The first point is a matter of arguing the merits of one theory as a guide to policy rather than another. The second point is a matter of fact — and has now been conceded by NIESR:

> The most serious error made in the various National Institute forecasts of personal incomes and prices has been the tendency in recent years to underestimate inflation.

(Article by Mr A.J.H. Dean of the National Institute, in its Review of November 1976). Those who criticise NIESR for the inaccuracy of its forecasts *per se* miss the point entirely. What is wrong is not their inaccuracy, but their bias; and the Institute's refusal to acknowledge that there was any other way to run the economy except on the basis of such forecasts. Together with other institutions influencing 'informed opinion' NIESR thus encouraged governments in thinking they could 'get away' with a 'dash for growth', as seen above all in 1972-73. The biggest misunderstanding of all is to attribute the growth policy pursued at that time to the personal wishes of Tory leaders such as Mr Heath and Mr Barber. The whole point of this pamphlet is that such policies follow from the *climate* of economic opinion and of establishment thinking. Prime Ministers and Chancellors are influenced by this climate and snatch at the chance of following "popular" policies only when the ground has been prepared; when they have become "respectable" and are advocated by "respectable" newspapers.

The most interesting phases of the "dashes for growth", as of the "go-stop" cycle, for analysts of ideology, are the "stops". A characteristic of ideologies is that the belief itself must not be questioned: other reasons for failures must be found. Given the complexity of economic data, and Britain's openness to international influences, this has never been difficult; at least until 1975. The excuse advanced depends of course on the particular interest that needs to be defended within the overall "growth" ideology. Officials at the Treasury were never at a loss. They could say with truth that they never believed in "growth" anyway, and imply that the experiment had only been a political expedient to lower unemployment in the run up to a general election (1955, 1959, 1964, 1974). They could then revert to their "true" Gladstonian function as guardians of fiscal responsibility — garnished with whatever economic doctrine happened to be around at the time. This was once provided by the "Paish thesis" of the need for a "margin of spare capacity", and it looked in 1974-75 as if "monetarism" might come in handy. Either way, the Treasury can sit back and imply that what went wrong was a lack of control over government expenditure — and lo and behold, here was the Treasury only too willing and anxious to control it. A proper sociological analysis would, in my view, reveal a different story; that the Treasury has acquiesed in experiments in growth — partly because of sensitivity to previous criticism, partly because it has sometimes been infected with the current optimism and partly because the net result would probably be an increase in the size of the public sector and thus in its power. Unfortunately, such commonplace "economic" accounts of institutional behaviour — that they, like individuals, behave in such a way as to maximise their interests — still strike the English as being in bad taste (indeed often as incomprehensible).

The Treasury enjoys the advantage of not having its views on the record, since it is supposed to be the creature of ministers. Growth doctors who wear their hearts on their sleeves have a harder time explaining away failure. Politicians can say that "the private sector let us down". But true growth men could not exactly say that, because they had proclaimed that growth in demand was just what the private sector wanted. Instead, they usually blamed the Treasury. Here, too, they followed in the footsteps of Lord Keynes. But that really lasted only for the 1950s; thereafter this excuse for failure was succeeded by "the virility symbol" of the pound sterling and its "economically illiterate" supporters in the City. The City itself, which numbers far more growth advocates than is generally allowed, blamed excessive government spending.

The failure of the 1972-73 dash for growth required new excuses from all concerned. The alibis used on previous occasions would not do, because the Treasury had plainly gone along with expansionary policies, government spending overseas had been controlled, the pound sterling had been left free to float, and the City had willingly provided all the finance needed to fuel the growth of demand. The difficulties on the latest occasion of keeping the ideology intact probably explain why so many people have crossed over to the "monetarists". Yet as urged above, *ad hoc* monetarism is not enough. The old habits could easily return under a new guise. Even now there are many who insist that the collapse of policy was the result of the miners' strike in January – February 1974 and the increase in oil prices (the new alibis). Thus it is more than ever necessary to explain why British policy remained – much more than that of any other country – in the grip of a damaging ideology and conflicting institutional pressures for so long.

3. The Formation of Policy

IN the usual portrayal of the process through which macro-economic policy is determined, the main influences are assumed to be those of the government's economic advisers on the one hand and political pressures on the other: two influences that may be labelled "Science" and "Politics". The economic advisers are assumed to be relatively objective, basing their policy recommendations on the best forecasts available to them about the likely movement of the economy and then recommending a stimulus or restraining action according to the view taken as to whether effective demand is likely to exceed or fall short of the rate of growth of productive potential. Political pressures then come into the picture in the form of electoral commitments, Cabinet struggles, international obligations, the mood on the back-benches in the House of Commons, the views of the Confederation of British Industries, the Trades Union Congress, the City and other lobbies. The Chancellor's annual budget judgement as well as other overall measures of economic policy are seen as the product of these possibly conflicting pressures.

Economists will tend to assume that the most important influence on policy is the economic theory on which it is based; bad policy is the result of bad economics. Politicians and political observers will tend to assume that political considerations are uppermost − leading often to the cynical view that policy could not have been any different. A sociologist would regard both views as *simpliste.*

To start with "Politics": political pressures are in fact not so strong in the field of economic policy that the Chancellor and his advisers are deprived of effective freedom of action (although strong conviction may be required to stave down the well orchestrated clamour about the unemployment statistics). Usually, the Chancellor has a very wide margin of room to exercise his own judgement. There are many reasons for this, not least the fact that the effects of any misjudgement are seen only after a long time-lag, and even then those holding different theories about the proper course of policy will continue to dispute the wisdom of any particular policy decision. Rarely has the Chancellor's overall "budget judgement" (as distinct from particular taxes) been substantially modified in the course of the Parliamentary debates about the Budget.

As for "Science", a wide range of opinions is in fact held by responsible people about what to do in any given situation because of differences of view both as regards the proper objective of policy and as regards the economic theory used to guide policy. Arguments about economic policy are in effect conducted by appealing to the reader to consider interpretations of facts or recommendations about policy *as if* the theory underlying them were proven and the objectives agreed. "Let us so manage the growth of monetary demand *as if* we were sure that a high pressure of demand will encourage long-term growth"; or "Let us impose an incomes policy *as if* we knew that this will curb inflation"; or "Let us keep the growth in the money supply to some pre-determined rate equivalent to the estimated long-term up-trend in output *as if* we were sure that any attempt to spend ourselves into fuller employment was doomed to fail".

In truth, economics is not able to tell us how to run the economy, even if the objectives of policy are regarded as given. This is mainly because, as society changes, so do its problems. To be sure, as Sir Donald Macdougall has reminded us, the uncertainty attached to economic forecasts is no reason in itself for trying to do without them:

> In my view the rational way to make decisions is to base them on the likely range of possible outcomes, with a different range being given for each possible outcome. (Sir Donald Macdougall, Presidential Address, Royal Economic Society, 27 June 1974, published in *The Economic Journal,* December 1974).

But is even such a modest view of forecasting sufficiently modest? Who or what determines the selection of economic theories on which the forecasts of different possible outcomes are to be based? However far back the economist steps, can he dissociate himself from the assumptions of his group, or from a preference for one theory over another? Cannot any policy recommendation be challenged, not only because of the uncertainty attached to future events in society but also because of legitimate disagreements about the appropriate theory to select for the purpose in hand and the problem to be solved?

It is important to stress that neither politics nor economics can be regarded in any simple way as determining policy because it has become too easy to rule out policies on the grounds of their "political unacceptability". It has become commonplace amongst those who see an inherent conflict between the political and economic "market places" to assert that, as a matter of practical judgement, levels of unemployment required in a non-coercive system to cure inflation – or in the long run to prevent hyper-inflation – are or will prove to be unacceptable. (This is a judgement that already incorporates any help that, some may think, can be received from a voluntary incomes policy – in the end the gains from any co-operation on that front will be eaten up by the operations of the contradictions in the system). Those who suggest deflation as a means of curing the problem, in the long-term, are in this conventional view just not being practical. But would not Keynes himself have asked: whence comes this practical judgement of the practical man?

Four points may be considered. First, nobody can really know what level of unemployment is politically unacceptable – given the alternative of accelerating inflation – and the more vehemently they assert their opinions, the more suspicious one may be. Secondly, the levels of unemployment regarded as economically feasible are continually *changing.* In 1937, Keynes had advocated measures to restrain the boom when unemployment was well above one million; in 1943, in the discussions preceding publication of the White Paper giving the government's historic commitment to high and stable levels of employment he noted that there was "No harm in aiming at 3 *per cent* unemployment, but I shall be surprised if we succeed"; Sir William Beveridge himself in his Report in 1942 mentioned 8½ *per cent,* adding "it would not be prudent to assume any lower rate". In the 1950s, as policy appeared to succeed, the feasible level was brought down from 3 *per cent* to about 1.5 *per cent,* a figure which then became a political target for maximum unemployment; since then the politically "unacceptable" level has been revised upwards to 5 *per cent.* Thirdly, there was not in fact much evidence in 1974-76, when unemployment throughout the world climbed to levels that would have been considered unacceptable if inflation had not been perceived to be a greater threat, of political turbulence or even much social discontent. The elections in the autumn of 1976 in Sweden, Germany and the United States yielded a shift to the centre – or even right-of-centre – instead of a swing to the left, suggesting popular endorsement of anti-inflationary measures. Fourthly, the work done on the unemployment statistics themselves (in particular John Wood, *How Much Unemployment?,* IEA Research Monograph 28) was effective in persuading some ministers and their advisers who are after all the only people who actually *make* policy – as distinct from the electorate which votes for parties – that the social and economic significance of the figures had changed, so that the *political* significance of the figures was beginning to change also.

It should not be assumed that the voters will tend to vote for policies that bring ultimate destruction just because in the short run they can be promised seductive assurances. Such evidence as is available suggests a more hopeful conclusion, even if some British eyes are now so jaundiced that they see the British disease spreading ineluctably to every corner of the globe.

A better approach to the question: "What determines the climate of opinion in which economic policy is formulated?" is to look at the main institutions which influence that climate, together with the aims each of them espouses in practice: See table overleaf. The absence of a tick in any particular column is not intended to imply that no institution cares about it (obviously they would all like to have ticks in every column); just that in fact their behaviour and/or policy recommendations shows it is not in the *forefront* of their concerns – in the sense that they are not prepared to sacrifice their other aims for it. Other people would rearrange the ticks little; but I question whether exhaustive research and analysis would radically alter the general picture.

	Growth	Sterling	Full Empl.	Stable Prices	Preference for results in Short term	Long term
Politicians	✓		✓		✓	
The Bank of England		✓			✓	
The NIESR	✓		✓		✓	
NEDO	✓		✓			✓
The TUC	✓		✓		✓	
The CBI	✓				✓	
The Economist	✓		✓		✓	
The City		✓		✓	✓	

The conclusions to be drawn from the table are that *growth* and *full employment* head the list as the aims shared in common by most, with *sterling* third and *stable prices* having no powerful lobby that makes its attainment its principal aim. Any of the above institutions might query this judgement, I admit. Yet I challenge any observer of the British economic scene over the past 20 years to try to prove that the objective of stable prices has been championed by any of these influential bodies. Politicians have been sidetracked from it by the over-riding commitment to full employment since the Beveridge White Paper; the Bank of England, a natural candidate for champion in this regard, was partially diverted by its preoccupation with sterling (not a good proxy for internal price stability, even under a fixed exchange rate, for two reasons; first, because all kinds of expedients can be used to prop up its external value whilst domestic prices rise − borrowing, running up liabilities to other sterling countries, exchange controls etc; secondly, because the Bank's championship of *sterling* left it vulnerable to charges of holding up *growth*). Thus the focus of debate was shifted away from *price stability* v *full employment* to *sterling* v *growth*.

None of the others have consistently put stable prices at the top of their policy aims. Most of them argued that it could be secured as an ancillary result of policies designed fundamentally for other purposes – incomes policies designed to keep *incomes* down so as to maintain full employment or growth, or in the case of the City, deflationary policies designed to secure *sterling*, so that outward foreign investment and the other activities it holds dear might continue unimpeded.

The ticks against the question: "which institution puts long-term consideration against short-term ones?" are equally hesitantly placed. Nevertheless, the general impression – that nobody cares very much about the long-term fulfilment of any of these aims – is surely indisputable. (True, the great Keynes dismissed the long-term with his caustic comment about long-term mortality. Yet this is yet another of his *obiter dicta* that has been taken more seriously than he ever intended). The suggestion made here is that the short-term bias of policy has been unduly aggravated in the process of policy formation by the institutions influencing that policy.

NEDO has some claims to be considered; its early reports, and the work of the little Neddies for particular industries, might have achieved something in a stable economic environment. However, given the climate of opinion during these years and especially in the early 1960s, when the Treasury and the Bank were thought to be stopping Growth (*The Economist,* 14 April 1962 "The most cursory enquiry from the doorman at the Treasury, would inform NED in which rooms and behind which desks the main impediments to growth are sitting"), it swallowed the doctrine that the prior need was to ensure that monetary demand kept on rising. Indeed, the NEDC and later the Department of Economic Affairs under George Brown (now Lord George-Brown) were set up to provide countervailing centres of influence to the Treasury: worse, the Treasury itself was so impressed with criticisms of its own policies that it prepared the first paper for Neddy on obstacles to growth! However, the result in practice was that these institutions became embroiled in short-term tactics and the habit of short-term thinking. They identified "economic growth" with the upswing in the business cycle – from a previous spell of "underemployment" to one of "full employment". The Bank of England is another institution which might have been expected to take a longer term view; but its preoccupation with movements in the financial markets gave it, too, a short-term time horizon.

Following chapters look in more detail at the behaviour of, and influence exerted by, some of the main institutions identified in this chapter, starting with the Bank of England, and then turning to the "growth doctors" themselves, notably the National Institute of Economic and Social Research and *The Economist*.

4. The Fifth Column at Work

The Bank

THE Bank of England has played a vital role in the development of British economic policy — a much larger role than its subsidiary position as the agent of the Treasury in many fields would suggest. First, its international prestige and historical pre-eminence amongst the world's central banks have lent an air of gravity to its views not only on international monetary questions but also on domestic affairs and policies. Secondly, its active participation in financial markets backed by its technical expertise has enabled it to claim a special insight into those intangible factors that can make or break a financial policy: confidence, the mood of the markets and the attitudes of holders of sterling overseas or of gilt-edged stocks at home. Thirdly, its views on policy questions have been informed by those of the private-sector institutions in the City of London — and no government can now ignore the contribution made by the City to the surplus that Britain regularly notches up on the "invisible" account. Fourthly, the Bank has over the past 15 years developed a lively economics department which again has strengthened its voice in the counsels of government.

The Bank's influence and expertise have come together to exert a strong influence in two specific areas of policy: the management of sterling and policy towards interest rates. In both areas, the ostensible policy has changed: from fixed to floating exchange rates, and from rigid to flexible interest rate policies. In both areas, however, the underlying constraints on policy, the largely subconscious framework of attitudes and assumptions with which this paper is concerned, continued to influence policy making.

The defence of sterling has been the Bank's major preoccupation since the war. Between 1949 and 1967 it successfully held the exchange rate within a narrow band at $2.80, whilst re-establishing external covertibility in 1959 after dismantling the war and immediate post-war exchange controls. After devaluation to $2.40 in 1967, the Bank again held the line until 1971 when, between 20 August and 19 December, the pound was allowed to float — the parity being re-established at a higher dollar value (roughly $2.60) at the latter date. On 1 May 1972 sterling joined the *"snake"* system linking EEC currencies and some others, but left it on 23 June, since when the pound has floated down to $1.60 (October 1976).

There were both intellectual and "moral" reasons for this preoccupation. Intellectually, the Bank was convinced of the technical case for fixed exchange rates — as were other central banks and economists — after the war, when the memories of the floating exchange rates and multiple-currency practices of the 1930s were still fresh. Morally the Bank was very conscious of its obligations to its overseas customers — holders of sterling in the overseas sterling area and elsewhere. This sense of moral obligation reinforced its aversion to currency depreciation and its acute awareness of the significance of confidence factors in currency movements to make it view with horror any public discussion of devaluation. Yet the Bank was also persuaded, partly out of a feeling of guilt that it had been in some measure to blame for the unemployment of the 1930s, of the new Keynesian approach to employment policy and the economists whom it hired were of this school of thought. The notion that domestic monetary policy should be used to secure sterling was turned into its opposite: that maintenance of the pound's external value was a way to ensure domestic price stability without damaging employment.

Now, we are told, anybody who cares to ask can discover that for several years — indeed, more or less since floating in 1972 — official policy has been to let the pound depreciate in the exchange markets so as to reflect Britain's domestic inflation rate, thus maintaining the price competitiveness of British goods overseas. But the fact is that the measures used previously to maintain the pound's external value are still in force. Exchange controls remain as tight as ever and the Bank has acquiesced in the Treasury's policy of further borrowing overseas—borrowing sums far greater than were ever contemplated

26

under the old fixed-exchange-rate regime. So the current balance of payments plunged more deeply into the red in 1974-75 than ever before. Nobody forced Britain to take on this indebtedness (if other countries wished us to support sterling for their own reasons they could have been requested kindly to put up the money and mortgage their own future earnings for the good cause). There were many other options available, such as floating freely, or restraining home demand sufficiently.

Old habits lived on in the authorities' handling of the gilt-edged market as well. From the point of view of overall economic policy, the gilt-edged market fulfils a vital function, for the sale of gilt-edged stock to the general public is the main way in which the authorities can finance a budget deficit without adding to domestic credit and (other things being equal) the money supply. The usual way in which a seller tries to persuade a potential buyer to take his goods is to offer him an attractive price; a low price for a gilt-edged stock means a high interest rate. But the Bank has never been willing to accept the logic of the market-place as applied to the gilt-edged market. The forces of supply and demand brought into balance by the price mechanism might apply to every other market in the world, but please not to the currency markets or the gilt-edged market. The Bank maintained, against its critics, that the reaction of the market to falling prices (rising yields) might be "peverse" and that to force sales on a falling market would carry the danger of "demoralizing" it. Another moral issue. (Economists would at this point explain the complex issues involved in the debate about whether the size of the national debt or other factors meant the Bank's views were right; all I am concerned to point out is that there is another view — and that the policy actually followed necessarily had certain effects).

Again, we are now told that the authorities have become much more flexible — a change that preceded the introduction of the new technique of credit control in 1971 (Competition and Credit Control). A corollary of this new technique was indeed that the authorities would pay more attention to movements in the monetary aggregates (not exclusive attention, to be sure, but more attention than formerly), and would accordingly have to accept fluctuations in interest rates required to control these aggregates. But once again, the conversion was far from whole-hearted.

The authorities' continuing difficulties in accepting the logic of the market place were illustrated in an illuminating speech delivered by Sir Leslie O'Brien (now Lord O'Brien) in December 1970, ("Monetary Management in the United Kingdom", Jane Hodge Memorial Lecture.)

"It is not a simple matter in an inflationary age" said Sir Leslie,

> to judge the level of interest rates most appropriate to the thrust of policy; and the growth of the monetary aggregates may offer some guidance in this respect. But to focus solely on the money supply or DCE among the financial, let alone the economic variables, is not enough. It is essential to the understanding of monetary processes and their implications to look much more widely at the stocks of financial assets held throughout the financial sector – and indeed throughout the economy as a whole – and at the financial flows between all the major sectors. We have been concentrating much effort on this in the Bank and shall continue to do so.

He continued:

> In short, while we are keeping a watch on developments in the monetary aggregates, we are looking at them as guidelines for overall policy rather than as targets. I doubt whether it would be possible to force through a pre-determined volume of (gilt-edged) sales even at the cost of marked instability in interest rates; but even if it were possible, to attempt it would in many circumstances be both damaging and purposeless. For expectations play a large and unpredictable role in investors' decisions. Even when the government is running a large revenue surplus, maturities of nearly £2,000m. a year require careful handling if adequate refinance is to be forthcoming.

A few sentences later, however, the Governor said that:

> apart from the needs of Government finance, our main end is to achieve the degree of monetary restraint judged to be appropriate to the economic situation and the overall direction of policy. Any particular degree of restraint in any particular circumstances will involve a certain pattern and level of interest rates which will have to be accepted.

All the ingredients in the Bank's traditional approach to monetary policy are contained in those lines. The seeds of the

1972-74 monetary explosion were already sown. The stress on the need for "careful handling" brought in the Bank's role as market operator, the weight of its expertise; the emphasis on uncertainty and the unpredictability of investors' reaction to falling prices gave it the rationale for supporting the market (creating liquidity) even while in the same breath the Governor was acknowledging that "any particular degree of restraint" would involve a level of interest rates that "had to be accepted"; the warning that it was "not enough" to look at the money supply or DCE prepared the ground for a period when the volume of money in the economy was to *double* without the Bank feeling at any point that it should make a stand against government policy. "Complexity", "careful handling", "uncertainty", and subservience to the "overall direction of policy" (i.e. Treasury policy) – these have been the keynotes of the Bank's approach to monetary policy for a generation.

So in 1972-73 the Bank again pegged interest rates for a period, gilt-edged securities were not sold to investors in sufficient quantities and monetary expansion surged ahead. This time, the main reason given was that the government was embarking on a strategy to raise the long-term rate of growth. The Bank of England wished to be seen to be playing its part to encourage investment, so it held down interest rates (as indeed the Prime Minister was determined that it should). Again, the ostensible reason for intervention changed: the result did not.

The pegging of sterling and the pegging of interest rates at levels decided by administrative fiat rather than the market reacted on each other. For the only monetary means available to economic policy-makers if they wish to influence the price level, and thus secure the strength of sterling, is offered by the possibility of influencing the volume of credit created in the economy. And the only instrument available for controlling the volume of credit through market forces is the rate of interest. To peg the rate of interest is thus, in effect and in the long run, to lose control of the rate of exchange of sterling.

The Bank's distinctive approach is rooted in its history and its deep involvement in the markets. Because it has been such a good player, it is loathe to be just a referee. It takes a market man's view of the markets rather than an economist's and as mentioned above many of the economists it has chosen have been neo-Keynesians who are not enthusiastic about the role either of markets or of money in the economy. Its canny practitioners have thus joined hands with its newly-recruited economists in attributing the major ills of the economy — inflation, the balance of payments deficit, financial dislocation and crises — to causes which had nothing to do with monetary policy. The technical people had never seen the main importance of their operations in the government securities markets as that of determining the stock of money in the economy; and were not surprised to be told therefore by the bright economists that their operations were not only "very complex" (they knew that already) but had little or no economic significance. What really mattered, they could all agree, was whether the government could secure an agreement on an incomes policy with the trades unions. Hence repeated calls for such a policy in the Bank's *Quarterly Bulletin.*

The Bank has also encouraged the politicians' natural tendency to take a short-term view of events. This, too, stems from its roots in financial markets, where a day is a long time. Like the City around it, it prides itself on rapid adaption to changing circumstances. It has never put much faith in strategic policy objectives. Yet there are so few institutions in a modern democracy ready to take a long-term view that the central bank is one that should do so, and that is indeed the role it plays in many developed and developing countries today.

Monetary policy in Britain still appears to lack strategic objectives. A visitor to the Bank bent on discovering the authorities' view of monetary policy is readily given an account of recent interest rate movements, the intricacies of the Treasury bill tender, of the latest government stock offering and the impact of overseas rates. What he is not given (except when the IMF is at the helm) is a statement of the overall monetary expansion the authorities wish to see and how they intend to bring it about. Questions on this are answered with a shrug, as if that were to ask altogether too much of the Bank*. True, such overall policy targets would have to be set and disclosed by the Chancellor rather than the Bank; yet one cannot help suspecting that the Bank has been quite content to

---

*During 1976 quantitative monetary guidelines were publicly announced but it was not clear whether this practice would be maintained when the economic situation improved.

hide behind the Treasury's outmoded reticence. By contrast, a visitor to Frankfurt or Washington will be told that the policy to aim for a growth of 'X' *per cent* in the money supply, that this may mean interest rates going up to 'Y' *per cent* but at the same time output may be recovering and unemployment should fall to 'Z' *per cent* and the balance of payments move into a deficit/surplus of $Xm. Such targets are not usually hit spot on; the purpose of making them is not to be proved right, but to give a structure to discussion about policy and to policy itself.

The stress on the short term also shows through in the interpretation of monetary statistics. Through much of 1972-74, when underlying growth in the money supply was rapid, the Bank of England would each month stress the distorting factors at work — notably the various types of "arbitrage" transactions by companies taking advantage of marginal differentials in yields (distortions that were themselves mostly the result of the official policy of holding down rates). Warnings of this sort are fair enough. But not when used to obscure the steepness of the upward trend. In this case the figures lost the impact they might have had. Then, after 1973, the figures could be presented as showing a "slow-down" regardless of the fact that the increases were still high by any standards other than those of 1972-73. Between end 1971 and end 1975 Britain's money stock (M3) almost doubled; yet the emphasis on the short-term intrepretation of the figures allowed this to happen as the months went by, in almost an absent-mended manner. And as the money supply began to accelerate again in 1976 the Bank of England was once more quick to assert that the figures were distortorted by exceptional features.

History, geography and the personalities of successive governors have shaped the characteristics and concerns of the Bank and the special kind of influence it has exerted. The identification of the Bank with the age of Britain's supremacy in world trade has not even now faded from public consciousness. The revival of the City as the leading international financial centres certainly in Europe and possibly in the world (New York being the only rival), has enabled the Bank to keep intact its own status in the central banking fraternity, a status which in turn has sustained its domestic influence. A special aura of High Finance still surrounds the

Governor when he descends from his fortress in the heart of the City to tender his (usually bleak) advice to the Chancellor or Prime Minister of the day. But this prestige and this aura have not since the war been devoted to securing the domestic value of the currency by controlling the creation of money. Instead that objective has been sought by supporting the external value of the pound, whilst allowing excessive credit creation at home; and the inevitable result has been inflation and growing foreign indebtedness, not stable prices.

The criticisms of the Bank voiced in this chapter have been made often before. The first trenchant criticism of the authorities for setting an over-ambitious parity for sterling (the return to gold at the pre-war parity of 1925) was made by Keynes himself in the early 1920s, when another of his themes was the need for high interest rates to choke off a boom. That was indeed the time when British economic policy took the wrong turning — a turning into a quixotic land of dreams from which it has not yet woken. The great man knew what was wrong — an over-valued pound and an inflexible monetary policy. As Professor Harry Johnson has pointed out, he was led to invent his new economics as a second-best alternative at least partly because he could not persuade the Establishment of these truths. Fifty years later is it too much to hope that his original insights rather than his second-best alternative will gain acceptance?

NIESR and Others

The National Institute of Economic and Social Research has been·the most influential of the institutionalized ideologues of "growth". Its recommendations are always listened to with special attention because it is supposedly independent of the Treasury, yet uses the same forecasting techniques, and is thought to be on the "inside track", to know what is in the mind of top treasury officials. It has been described as a citadel of Keynesianism; I would prefer to call it a citadel of "expansionism". This section tells how it prepared the ground

for the boom that set the British economy back a generation.
"For some time now", NIESR declared testily in August
1970:

> we have been arguing that the outlook for domestic economic
> growth and for the external balance was such as to suggest both the
> need and the scope for a programme of phased reflationary action.

It argued that if existing policies were retained, the outlook
was for an expansion at an annual rate of no more than some
1.5 *per cent,* so far below the assumed rate of rise of productive
potential as to imply a further sizeable increase in
unemployment. The Institute dealt with the objections which
could be raised to its plea for reflationary action. (The term
"reflation" is used by NIESR in broadly the same sense as in
this pamphlet, i.e measures such as tax reductions or higher
public spending resulting in a rise in the flow of expenditures
and demand). These objections had to do with inflation, the
balance of payments and the "wide margin of error involved in
economic forecasts". It was suggested, said NIESR in August
1970, that if monetary policy were operated "according to a
rule by which the money supply is predetermined to grow at a
fixed rate", then this could "ultimately make the nominal
national income grow also at a fixed rate". The cost in terms
of unemployment was, however, unknown and the NIESR
concluded that this was "a highly uncertain and dangerous path
to follow". Incomes policies should be employed instead. If,
however, "the constraints on an effective (incomes) policy are
too heavy", it continued, then the exchange rate should be
varied "either in steps or continuously" to cope with the effect
on the balance of payments of the subsequent price inflation.

Thus NIESR's advice in 1970 to the newly-elected Conservative
government was to *reflate demand* so as to raise the prospective
increases in the growth of output from 1.5 *per cent* nearer to
the 3 – 4 *per cent* range (possible ways of doing this included
"full use of the regulator" to vary indirect taxes, relaxation of
hire purchase restrictions and "restraint of nationalized industry
price increases" to boost real consumption); to *float the pound;*
and to adopt an *incomes policy.* This was a time, it may be
recalled, when price inflation was about 7 *per cent,* the public
sector borrowing requirement was zero, the balance of payments
was moving into large surplus and the massive overseas debts of

over £3,000m. incurred during the periods of deficit from 1964 to 1968 were being repaid. Unemployment was 2.6 *per cent.*

The story of the next five years shows how official policy adopted each of NIESR's three main recommendations in turn; how inflation rose to 20 − 30 *per cent:* how the public sector borrowing requirement rose to a rate of £11,000m. per annum; how the balance of payments plunged deep into the red; how overseas assets were run down and debts accumulated to a total of some £12,000m.; how investment in manufacturing slumped; how, despite all the reflation of demand, unemployment never fell much or for long below the 1970 level even at the peak of the boom and subsequently climbed to 5.3 *per cent :* and how the Conservative government which had reluctantly adopted all these policies was voted out of office.

For anybody interested in grasping the pattern in events, the way in which the effects of policies built up over a period far longer than the time-horizon of forecasts made at the time, a detailed account of those ensuing years will be as unnecessary as it is distasteful. Everything that had happened in previous go-stop cycles happened again, on a bigger scale. The dynamic force in official policy − reflation as urged by the NIESR − was the same, and this time it was not checked by adherence to a fixed exchange rate for sterling.

The process took time. In November 1970 the Institute declared itself worried about inflation: "the most urgent problem for policy". This was when the consequences of the so-called "breakdown" in the Labour government's incomes policy − the big wage increases conceded in the winter of 1969-70 and first half of 1970 − were coming through into the indices for average earnings and threatening to fuel demands for yet bigger increases in the winter of 1970-71, when Mr Heath's new Conservative government was facing its first test. There are several competing interpretations of that "breakdown" in 1969 and the spring of 1970, to which many observers trace the beginning of the "wage explosion" of subsequent years. Keynesians naturally favour a "cost-push" hypothesis, resting on an assumed increase in union militancy resulting from unemployment, the rise in import prices after devaluation in 1967 and frustration with the incomes policy itself. Monetarists

34

are averse to such *ad hoc* explanations and frequently explain the rise in wages as an adjustment of UK costs and prices to the world level following the 14 *per cent* devaluation in 1967 — on the thesis that in a world bound together by fixed exchange rates any individual country has in the long run to follow the world inflation rate *plus* that required by any devaluations in which it indulges.

There is, however, another explanation, though admittedly of an *ad hoc* nature. To the present author at least it seemed clear at the time that the Prime Minister, Mr Wilson, had detected that he might lose the forthcoming general election, eventually held on 18 June, and that, realizing it was too late to stage a broadly-based economic recovery, he gave the green light to high wage claims instead — notably in the public sector: hence settlements such as the then unheard of 15 — 17 *per cent* increases for 220,000 industrial civil servants agreed between the governments and the unions on 12 June 1970.

But all monetarists agree that such wage increases, and the higher expectations they aroused, could not have led to a continued acceleration in the wage level unless "validated" by an increase in the money supply. In the public sector the government can of course both grant higher wages to its employees, behaving in this respect like a private employer, and print the money to pay for them, which a private employer cannot do. If it wishes to avoid the inflationary repercussion of such a policy, it can finance the higher wage bill in its own sector by raising taxation on the private sector or directing private savings into government gilts, thereby (either way) creating unemployment in that sector.

The NIESR expounded the Keynesian explanation. It went on to admonish the Chancellor, Mr Barber, for his reluctance to reflate. On 4 November 1970, Mr Barber told the House of Commons that:

> If one takes into account the continuation of the rapid rise in costs and prices which we have experienced over the past year or so, if follows that it would be wrong to take any steps likely to increase further the pressure of demand.

The NIESR replied haughtily that "for the scale of reflation we are envisaging . . . we doubt whether the risk of intensifying inflation is significant". Faster growth would lower cost pressures and help to moderate wage claims by fulfilling workers' expectations of increases in real incomes. A more vigorous incomes policy was required than the government's mild strategy of "leaning" on settlements in the public sector. By February 1971 the NIESR's recommendation had matured into a call for "a more or less explicit strategy for growth". But it was to be consumer-led:

> The consideration of timing points to an emphasis in the initial stimulus on raising consumption. Other sources of demand are likely to prove difficult to stimulate quickly . . . it is now doubtful whether any significant expansion of investment will occur until demand has been seen to be rising for some time.

A call for measures to raise investment − even if they be measures that start by raising consumption − is calculated to strike a responsive chord in the hardest heart. The possibility that investment might be encouraged by a policy that gave priority to price stability without controls was not considered. Instead, businessmen were regarded as rats, their animal spirits twitching to "stimuli" applied by students of their behaviour. (Any conception of businessmen as the intellectual equals of economists is foreign to the Keynesian tradition, which has put economists firmly in the cockpit of the national economy; NIESR at least had no intention of yielding its place there.)

Significantly, the Confederation of British Industries itself endorsed the National Institute's priorities. In February 1971 came the Rolls-Royce collapse and the Wilberforce award to the electricity supply workers. The government began to yield. Measures were taken in the budget in April estimated to raise growth, by 0.75 *per cent* by 1972, and then again in July (by a further 0.5 *per cent*) to an annual rate of about 4 *per cent.* All the same, NIESR claimed in August that unfortunately reflationary measures had been too long delayed, with the result that a downturn in investment had been "triggered off". NIESR welcomed the initiative by the Confederation of British Industries to limit voluntarily price increases to 5 *per cent* or less in the 12 months to July 1972, and the comparable restraint to be applied to the nationalized industries: steps which distorted the finances of both sectors (and created havoc in those of the nationalized industries) without securing restraint in wages.

36

In November the Institute discussed favourably the possibility of a "deliberate stimulation, for a brief period, of public sector spending": another nail was being prepared for the economy's coffin. By February 1972, NIESR had become strident in its advocacy of a big boost, despite conceding two points: first, that the rise in unemployment in 1971, though not planned policy, "probably had some part to play in tempering the accelerating tendency of inflation" and, secondly, that output was set to rise by about 3.5 *per cent* in 1972 without any further changes, i.e. as much as usually considered safe. That would stabilize unemployment, which reached a cyclical peak of 4 *per cent* in the first quarter of 1972, but would not, in NIESR's opinion at that time, bring it *down*. Committed to the notion that macro-economic policy can ensure the fulfilment of a pre-determined employment figure, NIESR snatched at a figure of 2.25 *per cent* as a definition of "full employment". A target growth rate of 5 *per cent* a year could accordingly be set for 1972-73, or an annual average rate of 4.5 *per cent* "over the next four or five years". Tax cuts of an unprecedented scale were suggested — a "revenue loss" of £2,500m. "The danger of overshooting has become remote".

In the event Mr Barber cut taxes (on an equivalent basis of measurement) by £1,600m. NIESR was rather pleased, though it would have liked more — it doubted whether a 5 *per cent* growth rate would be achieved (in the event GNP grew at an annual rate of about 8 *per cent* between the second half of 1972 and the first half of 1973 as the slack was taken up). Its May 1972 review welcomed the fall in unemployment in May which showed "that doubts about the effectiveness of Keynesian remedies for unemployment were unfounded". They should have waited.

The mood was encouraged by commentators such as Mr Peter Jay who, whilst pointing out in graphic language the risks and dilemmas faced by policy, made many statements such as the following on the 1972 budget:

"(The Chancellor) seems to have made a half or at most three-quarter-hearted stab at unemployment, while virtually ignoring the problems of inflation and the balance of payments . . . As to the need to avoid a purely ephemeral spurt leading to another stop, that is the language of the 1960s and has little application to a situation in which the economy is operating at least 7.5 *per cent* below its full employment capacity." *(The Times,* 22 march, 1972).

The way in which Mr Jay thought any problems should be tackled had been made clear many times; thus he complained on 17 March that "Both political parties seem unable to propose a fair, flexible and forceful pay policy". This was echoed in nearly all the "respectable" economic comment at the time, including the letter columns of *The Times.* Mr Peter Oppenheimer from Oxford University was in the forefront of those wanting an incomes policy (as in the London and Cambridge report published in *The Times* of 28 June). The August 1972 number of the NIESR review was largely devoted to the case for a tougher incomes policy, to flank the growth policy. The floating of the pound was favourably noted. This was the time when the press and informed opinion was more or less solidly behind the Barber strategy, whilst urging government to grasp the incomes policy nettle. *The Times* summed up the prevailing mood:

> A new incomes policy based on the cost of living and extending over a considerable period would, if it were successful, ensure the maintenance of our competitive position which the floating pound will serve to establish. That is now the one remaining element required for a long and steady improvement in the success of British industry and the prosperity of the British people (24 June).

Such is the infectiousness of the growth bug — such the euphoria it allows. To quote Professor John Vaizey (now Lord Vaizey), telling the readers of the *Sunday Telegraph* on 26 June 1972 how to interpret the floating of the pound:

> If I am correct, then, in arguing that economic growth is the supreme objective, and the means are capable of being changed, the floating of the pound is as much a master stroke as the 1972 budget was and as, in a different field, Mr Whitelaw's Irish achievement has been, an achievement strikingly similar to Mr Barber's in political economy. *De l'audace, et encore de l'audace, et toujours de l'audace,* as Mr George Thomson must have learned that Danton said.

But before this audacity met with Danton's fate, another bridge had to be crossed: the fateful consuming of political capital in the search for an incomes policy, *after* the essential political surrender to the unions had already been made in the winters of 1969, 1970 and 1971.

The November issue of NIESR's Review was overtaken by the Prime Minister's proposals for a £2 a week limit on all pay rises in return for a pledge for 5 *per cent* growth. The "tripartite talks" about this broke down on 3 November and were followed on 6 November by the Counter-Inflation Bill for a 90-day statutory pay/prices freeze, with provision for a 60-day extension, and a more complex stage 2. The proposals were widely applauded in the press, especially by *The Times* and of course by NIESR.

By February 1973 NIESR had revised its forecasts upwards at last. Thanks to higher public expenditure, which it had recommended, it now thought that the rate of increase in output would be brought "very near to the Chancellor's 5 *per cent*". But what had happened to the balance of payments and inflation?

NIESR had expected reflation to reduce the big surplus achieved in 1971; it had forecast (in February 1972) that the current surplus in 1972 would be about £900m. and that reflation on the scale suggested would reduce it to about £300m. (at an annual rate) in the first half of 1973. In the event the surplus almost ran out in 1972 and turned into a deficit of £835m. in 1973. The Institute settled for a policy of "wait and see", whilst pinning hopes on the success of the incomes policy: "it is most important that the incomes and prices policy should succeed". There was "no imminent resource clash": i.e. a simultaneous improvement in the balance of payments and rising consumption could be sustained: "This situation of course contrasts with those of the 1960s when "stops" had to be instituted in order to release resources for an improvement in the balance of payments". But not for long. Only three months later, in May 1973, the Institute changed its tune on this front too:

> "When all is said, however, the fact remains that the emergence of excess demand in different sectors of the economy is likely to pre-empt resources from exports and to suck in additional imports, in some if not all cases".

So NIESR scratched its head and came up with a really splendid idea: "If the anticipated investment recovery is to be realized, these resources must be taken away from consumption". That is, they must be taken away from the item which NIESR had spent the last two years trying to stimulate. But how to do it without a return to deflation? Thank goodness the incomes policy was working. Confidently, NIESR said that it was "already plain that both Stage 1 and phase 2 of the present prices and incomes policy have had considerable success on the wages front . . ." There was "no reason" why lower unemployment should strain it, if it was fairly operated. The structure was "robust". "To sum up, there is no reason why the present boom should either bust or have to be busted so long as the additional instruments of incomes policy and the floating exchange rate are retained". The Institute's irritation with gloomy commentators who insisted on comparing the boom with that of 1963-64 was clearly expressed in its assertion that it was "the existence of these instruments which differentiates the present expansion from the boom of 1963-64".

In August 1973, the Institution's review distinguished itself in two respects: first by attributing the growing external deficit and domestic inflation to the rise in import prices; second, by revealing its expectation that "on the whole" commodity prices should turn down. To be sure, each opinion was hedged about with "ifs" and "buts". What mattered was the encouragement given to the fashionable interpretation according to which British policy was not responsible for the sudden deterioration in the economic outlook. "A large part of this rise (in inflation) can be ascribed to the world price situation and its impact on our import prices, exacerbated by the effective devaluation of sterling". NIESR's was an analysis that cut into the sequence of cause and effect at an arbitrarily-chosen point. For instance, it attributed part of the increase in import prices and inflation to the fall in the exchange rate, without considering whether, or to what extent, the fall in the exchange rate itself was a product of internal expansionary policies (notwithstanding the fact the Chancellor Barber had specifically resorted to a floating rate in order to eliminate an obstacle to "growth"). Nor did it see any inconsistency in having welcomed the option of a floating exchange rate as enabling Britain's price structure and monetary policy to be independent of those of other countries and then, 12 months later, blaming internal inflation on "import prices". The views of those trying to argue a contrary view at that time were simply ignored. Only two years later in its review of November 1975, did the former editor, Mr J.A. Bispham, at last acknowledge that "of course" the higher prices paid in 1973 by UK importers "need not necessarily have led to more inflation in the UK".

"A monetarist might argue" he continued with reference to an article by Professor David Laidler in *The Banker* in October 1973 "that it was still open to the authorities not to allow the money supply to follow passively a further rise in the general price level". He forebore to mention that this was precisely the policy of restraint which most other countries were actually following in 1973, pretending to regard it instead as some extraordinary, extremist, monetarist idea. Mr Bispham maintained in his 1975 article that such a policy would have led to politically unacceptable levels of unemployment: a judgement, one might have thought, to be taken by those elected by the people for such purposes, rather than by economists, whose business it is to display the policy options open to the government.

By the autumn of 1973 NIESR was plainly worried. But in those days leading up to the oil-price explosion, the encouragement given by NIESR and the national press to the government's growth policies was of vital practical importance. No effective restraining action was taken, so the oil price rise at end-1973 hit the UK economy when it was most vulnerable. In addition informed public opinion had been taught that rising commodity prices were the main cause for our problems; thus the ground had been prepared for Britain's attempt to borrow its way out of the oil crisis and blame world prices when things went wrong. Policy remained expansionary in the sense that although the money supply began to slow down, domestic credit continued to expand rapidly.

As another observer has commented, British payments policy since the war has amounted to:

a continuous financing of external deficits . . . achieved by exploding the reserve constraint through bribery of private investors of internationally mobile liquid capital resources by means of the artificial manipulation of national interest rates (Dietrich K. Fausten, *The*

Consistency of British Balance of Payments Policies, ([Macmillan Press, 1975] p.147).

But in 1973 the NIESR was in no mood for critical self-examination. The mood was one of a determined show of outward confidence: "the rise in investment . . . is now beginning". There was no way in which it could have been stimulated except by the big boost to consumption in 1972, said NIESR defensively. The only area where policy could be criticised was in not introducing an incomes policy earlier.

In its discussion of incomes policies, NIESR tended to assume that such a policy only has to be introduced for it to work. Hence repeated statements like the following: "Partly because incomes policy was introduced rather late in the day, unit wage costs have risen by 8 *per cent* per annum". The fact that incomes policies have always faced immense opposition, sooner or later, and have never succeeded in any western country in the long-run, tends to be disregarded (a small parenthesis on p.5 of the November 1973 review is the only exception I have come across to this) not only by the NIESR but by other analysts such as the London and Cambridge bulletin which explicitly stated that "too much shall not be made" of this fact.

Cold feet in the summer; alarm in the autumn. In its November review NIESR scored a good initial debating point by recalling the views of those who, it claimed, had said 18 months before that unemployment could not be reduced in the short term by the usual "Keynesian" remedies because there was not enough capital available. This view had been "decisively refuted by events". "But now we are asked to believe the opposite — namely that the capital stock cannot be fully utilized because of a shortage of labour". (This ignored those who had criticized the boom from the outset, not because it would fail, but because it was all too likely to succeed).

Then came the confession: "our view *has* changed". Unemployment was coming down faster then NIESR had expected. Productivity assumptions had been over-optimistic. "Potential output looks as though it is around 2 *per cent* below our earlier expectations; the amount of slack is less than we had estimated". And on the incomes policy front "whereas in August we assumed that a severe Stage 3 of incomes policy stood a chance of slowing down the rate of inflation, we now think that the actual Stage 3 may *exacerbate* what was already going to be a higher price rise on account of higher oil and other world prices" (italics added). As for the balance of payments:

> The annual rate of deficit in the three months ending October 1973 was already running just short of £2,000m. Although we would no longer expect the balance to return to zero by the end of 1974, which we did in August, we would expect the strong movement towards balance to continue into 1975.

In the event the current deficit was £1,700m. in 1975 and was forecast to rise to £2,000m. in 1976. NIESR tied itself into knots trying to explain away its £1,750m. forecast revision for the balance of payments. The trouble, it implied, was not so much the increased price of oil as the irritating British *penchant* for foreign goods.

The November 1973 review was notable also for laying down the law on the proper way in which the world should deal with the balance of payments problems resulting from the oil price increase:

> All the oil importing countries must reckon that their current payments balances will worsen because of higher oil prices, and Arab oil producing countries will gain reserves proportionately. This development, again, should not be a reason for oil-importing countries to take deflationary action.

This was a recipe for exporting the British disease to the world at large, encouraging inflationary tendencies in every other country. In the event none of them took any notice. Instead they deflated in order to finance the real cost of the higher oil prices feeding through into higher spending on imports by oil countries. But NIESR's opinion was reflected in British policy and in countless speeches to international audiences by both Mr Barber and later by Mr Healey. Even on its own assumptions, this policy disregarded the effect on Britain of the actual policy of other advanced countries which was to get out of deficit as quickly as possible. Thus Britain (and Italy) were by 1975-76 left holding the lion's share of the OECD countries' aggregate deficit. The debatable opinion that British policy had been right in theory was surely insufficient recompense for the humiliatingly weak posture to which this policy reduced the UK economy in practice.

The Institute's February 1974 review developed the theme by arguing that other countries should allow Britain to run what it termed a "full employment balance of payment deficit" — an intriguing concept. One had heard of "full employment budget deficits" — meaning a deficit resulting from recession and required to stimulate activity — but a "full employment balance of payment deficit" was at that time novel. In Britain's case it probably approached infinity.

More important, the review acknowledged the failure of policy. "It is not often that a government finds itself confronted with the possibility of a simultaneous failure to achieve all four main policy objectives: adequate economic growth, full employment, a satisfactory balance of payments, and reasonably stable prices". What NIESR understandably omitted to mention was that this all-round failure followed a period when the government of the day had adopted every major recommendation that NIESR had urged.

In this condemnation of policies, it is vital to recall that in all essential respects the policies were failing well before the oil crisis and miners' strike at the end of 1973. Investment had been expected to turn up for several years — the whole point of stimulating consumption in the first place was because there was thought to be no other way of stimulating investment. Yet as the NIESR's February 1974 review ruefully acknowledged, "investment in manufacturing industry was already turning out last year to be below our earlier expectations". Prices were rising *faster* than they had done before the introduction of the counter-inflation policy. Meanwhile unemployment had been dropping so rapidly as to alert even the Institute to the likelihood of overheating in 1974. Then came the most abrupt "stop" ever: planned cuts in government spending announced by Mr Barber in December 1973 on top of the short-term deflationary effect of the oil price increase; and in March 1974 a deflationary budget by the new Labour chancellor, Mr Healey.

Yet the NIESR could not bring itself to recognize a "stop" when it saw one. Its theory had told it that this could not happen, therefore it hadn't:

At first sight, it looks as though the familiar "stop-go" cycle has returned, especially as the later stages of the growth period were marked by a very large deficit in the current account of the balance of payments. However, as was made clear by the former chancellor in his major reflationary budget of 1972, the most recent period differs from previous post-war experience in that a fixed parity for sterling has been abandoned. The end of the boom has not been brought on by a run on the pound but a combination of rather different circumstances: the unprecedented rise in commodity prices, the oil crisis and, finally, the miners' ban on overtime and strike and the introduction of three-day working.

Throughout, NIESR had its eyes fixed on one interpretation of post-war economic history and one theory of economic policy. But it was those who saw another pattern and preferred another theory who had predicted that the boom would fail, and who had insisted on drawing parallels with 1963-64 and other periods of "stop-go". On their interpretation, the dynamic element in policy was "go": fiscal or monetary stimulation. It is not necessary to be a monetarist to agree with this interpretation. This "go" phase would always be pushed to the limit − i.e. until the balance of payments sank too far into the red and/or the exchange rate fell too far or domestic inflation rates rose too much. The rate of unemployment at which these effects would start to show was inherently unpredictable. The abandonment of the fixed exchange rate would mean that this dynamic domestic policy would tend to push the exchange rate down, putting import prices up − so that inflation would appear to be imported. But in truth Britain would in those circumstances be *exporting* inflation rather than *importing* it, adding by its payments deficit to real demand in the world. Domestic inflation would have been all the greater if part of the increases in domestic credit (DCE) had not flowed overseas (being absorbed by imported goods) rather than building up further monetary pressure at home. Of course, the adverse movement in the terms of trade imposed a real cost. Higher oil prices meant lower real incomes. But there was no point in trying to postpone it indefinitely by overseas borrowing, apart from smoothing its effects somewhat by *temporary* limited financing. Contrary to all British projections the Middle East countries *did manage to spend much of their new revenues,* requiring real adjustments on the oil-importing countries. Finally, it was no use trying to stimulate an investment boom by boosting consumption, because this only led to well-founded expectations that the boom would be short-lived; and, by the time consumption was pressing against capacity there would not be room physically for the increase in investment and exports that would by then be required. A "stop" would be unavoidable. Hence the well-known fact that businessmen who hearken to official exhortations to "invest" are those who frequently become bankrupt as a result. This disregard of the effect of policy actions or announcements on the expectations of businessmen is a crucial flaw in Keynesian analysis. They know the "stop-go" game — and thus no longer increase investment during a "go" but just raise prices.

The next four years were spent clearing up the mess. Everything slumped. For anybody interested in the broad sweep of events, the details of such "slack" periods following booms are familiar. Official policy switches this way and that; some components of demand may keep up for a time, e.g. public spending or consumption; but the basic fact is that the economy is in slump and little can be done about it. Even the extent of the slump has been broadly determined, by the time it arrives, by such factors as the volume of indebtedness entered into during the boom (national, corporate, and personal indebtedness), the preceding rate of inflation and the international situation.

The National Institute spent much of its time during these years (1974-76) discussing the need for a new incomes policy, since the previous policy had been exploded by the miners. It also flirted with the notion of import controls. Most of its ruminations, unfortunately, fitted firmly into the tradition of wishful thinking:

> But suppose, somehow, one could be sure that average earnings would rise by no more than 5 *per cent* per annum from here on. At once unemployment could become a target of policy again. (February 1975, p.5).

In May 1975, NIESR forecast a rise of 25 *per cent* through the year in earnings and in retail prices. Mournfully, it recognized that in these conditions the budget could not be directed at the normal target of policy: full employment. The budget had shown that the government would not continue "to validate a rate of wage increase between 20 and 30 *per cent* per annum".

To be fair, the review struggled manfully to deal with a new world in which nominal monetary magnitudes had suddenly assumed as great a significance as "real" (or constant price) calculations — and one in which the measure of the impact of the budget was changing. No longer was it just a matter of the net change in taxation, but of such magnitudes as the public sector financial deficit. NIESR's analysis represented a small and uncertain step towards monetarism.

In August 1975, however, the Institute reverted to its more familiar role as a would-be carrier of the British disease. Like Mr Healey, it could not resist the temptation to lecture other, more successful, countries on the conduct of economic policy. At a time when the economies of the big countries, notably the United States and Germany, were in any case turning up (August 1975) the NIESR called for a concerted reflation. "In a world in which the levers are to hand to reduce unemployment the UK should make it clear that it cannot allow its unemployment level to be dictated indefinitely from outside". Casting the UK in the role of international disciplinarian was perhaps not the most convincing of parts NIESR could have chosen. Naturally NIESR welcomed the new "£6 per week maximum" incomes policy set out in the White Paper, *The Attack on Inflation.* It forecast a rapid deceleration in inflation; a big improvement in the balance of payments in 1975, continuing into 1976; growth more or less at a standstill; and unemployment reaching perhaps 1.5 millions by the end of 1976. The outlook, said the Institute, "has been presented as though we felt our usual degree of confidence in our forecasts." Those with experience of these forecasts must have been thankful that it denied that this was so.

The November 1975 review, coinciding with a change of editorship, marked a big change in approach; "the Government cannot, and should not, feel free to stimulate or permit a substantial reduction in unemployment from its present level" unless the rate of inflation came down. Even more revolutionary was its acknowledgement that "there must also be control of the growth of money and credit in the upswing." But the most far-reaching statement was the least dramatic at first sight:

> There is an important difference in the environment in which we are forecasting; it concerns expectations about policies. In previous

situations of high unemployment, most people could be fairly certain that the Government would take action soon, and probably based their own actions on this assumption. On this occasion, they can have no such certainty. It is at least a credible possibility that the government will take discretionary action, or alternatively that it could be prevented from doing so by the pressure of events. The difference in expectations could produce a different pattern of behaviour from those previously observed.

What the National Institute was really saying was that the end of the political *commitment* to full employment could lead in the longer run to *fuller employment* in fact because people would be more careful to avoid actions (such as excessive money wage claims backed by strikes) which might make them unemployed.

In 1976 there were therefore several intriguing questions for critics of NIESR: first, had it finally discontinued the practice of treating the outlook for inflation mainly as a postscript to or derivative of its "real" forecast? Would it acknowledge that the time lags in the response of unemployment to movements in output (up to two years) plus the well-known inherent limitations in the forecasting method create a presumption for giving alternative guides to policy (such as that the money supply should at all costs be kept below certain maximum growth rates) at least equal consideration in policy recommendation to that of the prospective unemployment rate itself? Had it taken resolute action to remove the persistent inflationary bias in its own estimates and forecasts? Would it take a longer-term view in future, even if that entailed discarding much of its forecasting apparatus? These questions had not received an answer at the time this study went to press

The Economist's Economics

WE have seen that economic policy has been strongly influenced by the ideas and policy recommendations of identifiable institutions. These ideas and recommendations have had their greatest impact as much in the formation of a climate of opinion amongst "practical men" about the right thing to do as in influencing particular decisions. They have encapsulated the following notions:

1. Economic growth can be encouraged in the long as well as the short term by maintaining the pressure of demand at a high level;
2. Any resulting inflationary pressures can be curbed by an incomes policy;
3. Balance of payments difficulties can also be corrected by an incomes policy (which will restore competitiveness to British goods) or failing that by depreciation of the currency;
4. The pound sterling should be pegged from time to time above the levels to which undisturbed forces of the market would deliver it, to avoid "adding to domestic inflation" or "upsetting the international monetary system";
5. Interest rates should be pegged from time to time below the levels they would reach if control of the money supply were a real policy priority in order to "preserve an orderly market" to "encourage investment" and to "keep growth going";
6. The levels of unemployment which would be necessary to cure inflation through an old-fashioned deflation would be politically unacceptable;
7. If policies resulting from a government following these notions fails, the fault is the short-sighted militancy of the trade unions, wrong policies pursued by other countries or "acts of God" such as unpredictable surges in world commodity prices;
8. In those circumstances the right thing to do is to press on regardless, secure in the knowledge that Britain is the only country in step.

Nowhere were the main ideas in this list, notably the first three, argued more passionately and persuasively than in the pages of *The Economist*, a growth doctor second only to the NIESR in terms of influence on policy. Let us pick up the story in 1962. In April of that year *The Economist* told its readers that:

> Britain will not recapture its dynamic until the Chancellor gets himself a definite annual target for national economic expansion, and recognises that various pressures that now influence his policy — including his private urge to look respectable before certain circles in The Treasury, the Bank, the Cabinet, the trade unions, and (as he

mistakenly envisages the place) Zurich — must yield priority to his forward drive for attaining that expansion.

This was the time when Britain was becoming acutely alarmed at its continuing poor performance in the international growth league tables. The answer, it was believed, was to be found in the new system of "planning" copied from the French *Commissariat au Plan* combined with rapid monetary expansion. Growth would be self-sustaining if only enough people believed in it. Industry was asked to do its part, whilst the Government would do likewise.

No matter that Britain had never sustained a long-term growth rate anywhere approaching 4 per cent. If Chancellor Selwyn Lloyd would only commit himself to that objective firmly enough, the obstacles would be swept from his path:

> The most cursory inquiry from the doorman at the Treasury would inform Ned in which room and behind which desks these main impediments to growth are sitting (April 14 1962).

"Ned" — the newly-formed National Economic Development Council — was the knight in shining armour who would free the maiden of the British economy from the Gradgrinds and Bounderbys of the Treasury, the City, Zurich and the Cabinet. There were no real obstacles to faster growth; it was all in the mind.

By 1963, *The Economist* was chafing at the bit:

> There are only two policies from which (the Government) can logically choose. One possibility is to hold down expansion in order to hold down imports; this choice means continually delaying re-expansion from one year to the next . . . The other possibility is to start now to allow domestic demand to expand up to the edge of the point (a much more distant point than the Treasury's experts have hitherto realized) when it genuinely does begin to suck resources out of export markets; and meanwhile to take the strain of restocking import and of foreign bankers' nervousness either on the reserves . . . or on the exchange rate, or by raising interest rates. . . .

It should be noted that *The Economist* was much more ready to discuss financial policy, including exchange rate and interest rate policy, than NIESR, which hardly ever mentioned either of the subjects in those days. But it was all in the cause of expansion, ever-faster expansion; Mr Maudling's 1963 budget, giving tax concessions whose cost in a full year was unprecendentedly large, was received with faint praise: "Half speed ahead" ran the gloomy headline: "(The) £269 millions of tax reliefs for 1963 − 64 fall near to the bottom of the range recommended in these columns".

But, what happened then? The result of Mr Maudling's reflation to "do the Government's part" (as he put it) in achieving the target of the 4 *per cent* annual average rate of growth "which we have already accepted in the National Economic Development Council" was that demand spurted ahead, the balance of payments dived into the red and by 11 April 1964 even *The Economist* was acknowledging ruefully: "For the very short time ahead which it is possible to see, one would expect demand upon resources to continue to rise too rapidly in Britain".

Many people since have drawn the conclusion that the failure to devalue the pound was all that was wrong with the "growth" strategy of 1963 − 64. But *The Economist,* though plainly troubled and in two minds, knew where its duty lay: "The Government deferred not only to domestic political considerations but also, and equally, to the feeling of foreign and City bankers in, rightly, ruling out devaluation . . ." (28 November 1964, after the sterling crisis).

There followed a period of several years during which no clear consistent recommendations emerged from *The Economist* except that it wanted what it euphemistically called "big export incentives" buttressed by a "stern incomes policy". This was the period during which Mr Wilson, the Prime Minister, banned any mention of devaluation in Whitehall, and most newspapers took the cue, as they will do when matters of the utmost national importance are thought to be involved (though *The Economist* did mention it from time to time). Throughout 1965 and 1966 the economy continued to operate at a remarkably high level of activity; the "National Plan" came and went; but soon everybody was kicking their heels waiting for devaluation. When it arrived in November 1967, *The Economist* said that the announcement had been awaited "with a natural assumption that a compulsory wage freeze (at least on central trade union bargains) would be reimposed". It was a "numbing shock" to realize that this was not to be. It did however on this occasion press for a proper deflationary budget to make room for the anticipated increase in exports. And it got both the incomes policy and deflation in Mr Jenkins' 1968 Budget. *The Economist* approved, in general; indeed this was one of rare periods in post-war economic history when expansionists and "sound money men" were basically in agreement about the proper course of policy. Gradually this policy brought results. For a year or two it began to look as if British economic management really had changed its spots.

Signs of impatience were not long in reappearing at *The Economist* however. On the April 1969 budget judgement it reflected that

> The central forecast is that Britain's real gross domestic product will be rising at only a sluggardly annual rate of under 1.5 *per cent* during the current half year . . . and will then rise by only 2.9 *per cent* between this first half of 1969 and the first half of 1970 . . . Unless exports rise quite magically . . . the shattering political implications is that the Government will be trying to bring about some small further increase in unemployment over the whole period between now and the middle of 1970, when the election campaign will be well under way. (19 April 1969).

This is indeed what happened — a tribute to Mr Jenkins' political courage or the influence of our creditors at the International Monetary Fund. If it had not been for the (politically-inspired) "collapse" of the incomes policy — i.e. the beginnings of the wage explosion — encouraged by the Labour Government in the run up to the election in 1970 it would have handed to the Tories an economy poised for gradual expansion: competitive, balanced and clear of overseas short-term debts.

As it was the incoming Government played down growing signs of higher unemployment for nine months, and then began to apply bigger and bigger stimuli to the economy with panic repetition. *The Economist,* at least, had no qualms; its advice to Chancellor Barber for the March 1972 Budget was blunt:

> *The Economist* had several times set down its recommended strategy for next week's budget. Mr Barber should go for 5 *per cent* annual growth, even though this will bring balance of payments trouble before the end of 1973 . . . Reliefs of £2.5 billions would not necessarily lead to huge demand-pull inflation. . .(18 March 1972).

The following week, after Mr Barber had at least gone half-way to meet it, *The Economist* was judiciously approving:

Mr Barber's tax reliefs of £1.2 million in 1972-73 are predicated on the assumption that they will raise Britain's annual growth between now and the first half of 1973 from the 3 *per cent* which the Treasury would otherwise have forecast to the *5 per cent* which *The Economist* has kept urging as the right target rate.

One year later, the tone had become more strident; subscribers to the 31 March, 1973, issue were told that "The optimist is right to celebrate. On his view, which seems the more plausible, Britain is no longer on the brink of an economic miracle, but right in the middle of one . . ." And one week later:

better to play the growth strategy and deal with the problems that it throws up than to settle once more for the worst growth rate in the developed world . . . A vote of confidence in faster growth is not only Mr Heath's one plausible electoral strategy but also the country's greatest social and psychological need.

Enthusiasm for growth naturally went hand in hand with belief in the efficacy of the prices and incomes controls into which the Government had somersaulted the previous autumn. To help things along *The Economist* was able on 21 April 1973 to assure its readers that the rise in import prices was over:

the one card the Government has to play is that the rate of inflation through higher import prices is likely to slow during 1974. This is a very conservative and uncontroversial statement. All we are saying is that the 20 *per cent* rise in prices of imported materials and fuels over the past six months . . . will not continue at a rate of 20 *per cent* per six months; *The Economist's* own guess is that import prices of raw materials might actually fall from now on, so that the relief to the retail price index after about next November could be considerable.

Some people, however, were worried by signs of a rapid acceleration in the money supply. Not so *The Economist* which had:

already spelled out the reasons for thinking that the outsized increase in the money supply on the wider definition (M3) in recent months was exaggerated . . . one danger was that the authorities would go on forcing interest rates too high, as indeed they did for a time. That mistake has been corrected and some of the worst distortions in the interest rates structure have been ironed out. The job of financing the borrowing requirement without fuelling further large increases in the money supply is already a lot easier (21 April 1973).

By May, *The Economist* was becoming euphoric:

> The exciting thing about the present outlook is that investment and exports now look like taking off just as the consumer boom looks like fading . . . The prize of an economic miracle could lie so close to the Prime Minister's hand . . . The worst thing the Government could do is follow the advice of the fainthearted and introduce a demand-deflationary budget in the summer or autumn . . .
>
> Britain is running for tops in the European growth league this year, and is now enjoying its best boom since the war . . . Imported inflation is hurting Britain as everybody else, but we are dealing with it better than most.(5 May 1973).

So it went on.

> Britain is now in Europe. The pound is floating. The sterling area is being sloughed off. Growth is being sustained while a prices and incomes policy is in being. The restraint on wage and price inflation has survived its first serious challenge. There are signs that growth is now, in some part, becoming export-led. Britain is in a better position to keep its export prices competitive than many of its competitors are. The terms of trade seem more likely to remain steady, or improve, than they are to get worse. If the Tory party does not know what it wants to do with this considerable conjuncture of good judgement and good luck, it will indeed have lost the nerve to govern . . . (19 May 1973).

> With wage controls working, productivity racing ahead, the exchange rate floating, export prices competitive, world demand increasing, substantial spare capacity remaining, the consumer boom past, public spending reined back, and investment picking up, the present situation is without precedent. Mr Barber has shown he sees this. Nice one, Tony. Let's have another. . . (26 May 1973).

On through June and July:

> The worst could soon be over for the balance of payments (23 June 1973).

> Earlier this year the pessimists were predicting that the momentum of consumers spending would be maintained and that a deflationary Budget was needed. How clear it now is that they were wrong . . . (7 July 1973).

By this time, however, even *The Economist* could not entirely avert its eyes from events overseas. Foreign Governments with irresponsible objections to double-figure inflation were being brutish;

> In the upvalued currencies of Japan and West Germany some industrial commodities are actually cheaper than last year . . . British industry . . . seems to have been left gasping for breath whilst its West German competitors are busily shopping around, building up what are to them relatively cheap commodity stocks, and driving up world prices further, (14 July 1973).

> The least efficient and most right-wing economic policy today is being followed by the one nominally social-democrat government, Herr Brandt's Germany which, at a time when it is in large balance of payments surplus and should be upvaluing and expanding, is keeping its exchange rate fixed in the snake and meeting a cost-push inflation with the sort of liquidity squeeze that is threatening bankrupticies among quite big firms . . . The reason for this mess is that the Brandt government lacks the self-confidence to oppose a very conservative and not very sophisticated banking establishment in Frankfurt . . . (4 August 1973).

Fortunately the weekly's heroes kept their nerve, unperturbed by the way the predicted abatement in the surge of world commodity prices failed to materialize:

> Battered by an unprecedented surge in world prices of food and raw materials, and thus by a £1.3 billion annual rate of balance of payments deficit in the three summer months, Mr Heath is still not drawing back into stop-go. Mr Enoch Powell's call for the wrong policy of a swingeing autumn budget may now fortunately turn the Conservative establishment more firmly against it . . . (18 August 1973).

Still, some whistling was in order to maintain one's courage;

> The fall in the value of the pound has not been really justified in terms of domestic inflation. Britain has been more successful than most countries in controlling inflation and has been notching up some pretty impressive productivity gains on the way. A sterile relapse into stagnation has been avoided . . . The fact that it takes time for increased competitiveness to pay off is no evidence that it never will. So there is no need to scramble back to the funk-hole of high unemployment and slow growth that certain Labour critics and Mr Powell (and parts of the City) seem to be advocating . . . The problem facing the Government is one of timing. If it can hold the line on inflation at home, resources should increasingly move towards the balance of payments. Once the trade deficit clearly bottoms out, the going will improve . . . The last thing the Government should do is to reduce its chances by cutting real incomes through tax increases. (Same issue).

As events began to crowd in with the autumn *The Economist's* tone became more strident yet:

> The City establishment is much to blame for the strained relations between it and Mr Heath's Government. It has shown a singular lack of faith in the Government's economic policies ... (25 August 1973)

> Rarely has there been so little to criticize in (the Government's) management of the economy and rarely has it faced such an outcry – chiefly because it cannot control world prices. So the latest economic review of the National Institute of Economic and Social Research must have come as a considerable relief. Its careful and convincing analysis is in sharp contrast to what is being said in parts of the City and the media, encouraged by Mr Enoch Powell (1 September 1973)

As always, good times were just around the corner:

> The growth in demand is slowing down of its own accord, just as the Treasury and the National Institute *(and The Economist)* always said it would. The outlook is for 6.5 *per cent* growth this year followed by 3 *per cent* next. The problem of moving from a burst of speed to reduce unemployment to a sustainable expansion in line with capacity, without overshooting and creating excess demand, seems to have been solved for the first time since the war. There is therefore no domestic case for high taxes this autumn ... There is good news too on the external front. While the current deficit this year is likely to be around £1 billion, by the second half of 1974 Britain could be back in balance ... It is those who have been talking Britain into unnecessary panic who need to listen. Their behaviour could destroy continued growth. Britain is two thirds of the way to an economic miracle. (Same issue).

One week later:

> For the first time within memory, approximately the right economic policy is being followed from Whitehall. For the first time, the opportunity for a postwar economic miracle lies within our national grasp.

> The City had been expecting another set of bad trade figures on Thursday and it was not disappointed ... But the Bank of England has now joined the National Institute in forecasting better times to come. (15 September 1973).

The middle of *The Economist's* miracle ...

By the end of September the storm signals were at last getting through even to St. James's Street. The hunt was on for alibis:

> Some shortages are inevitable in the move to fast growth. Germany, France and Japan have all shown that high demand can go with limited inflation and a strong currency ... Meanwhile, despite

this year's public sector borrowing requirement, money has become both tight and expensive . . . if the Barber boom stops it will be for very different reasons from whose which ended Mr. Maudling's one. Most, but not all, of the present problems are caused by external events: world price inflation and the drift to restraint in Germany, Japan and the United States. (15 September 1973).

And how's this for wishful thinking?

By the end of 1974, inflation in Britain could be down to 5 *per cent* or less. Provided everything, especially the course of import prices, goes marvellously right . . . The terms of trade really could now rebound in our favour . . . Import prices will not level off, but could actually fall if world commodity prices go on sliding. (13 October 1973).

Thus *The Economist* was forecasting lower commodity prices in the midst of the biggest commodity price boom of all time and also industrial tranquillity on the eve of the most fateful industrial conflict in modern British history – and its policies depended on such forecasts.

Quite clearly most union leaders have no appetite for a fight. Mr Lawrence Daly, the miners' general secretary, called for a special TUC congress to decide how to attack stage three, but no other union leader at the meeting supported him . . . The prospect for the autumn is that it could be more peaceful than in any year since 1968. (20 October 1973).

Then on 3 November it suddenly transpired that there were signs of over heating:

Trains and buses are being cancelled daily. Even in the country, the coal mines are losing 500 men each week. The National Coal Board has lost 5 *per cent* of its labour force in the last six months. The employment exchanges have more unfilled vacancies than at any time for 22 years . . .

After a year of relative peace on the strike front, the air is thick with talks of strikes, go-slows and overtime bans . . . a conference of miners' delegates last Friday backed a call for an overtime ban . . .

One week later the incomes policy began to crumble:

The Home Secretary, Mr Robert Carr, said he was delighted by the news that a 19 *per cent* pay offer had ended the Glasgow fireman's strike on Monday. He should have been horrified . . . Stage Three's policy has a fatal woolliness. Its "flexibility" on which ministers keep congratulating themselves, is the flexibility not of steel but of putty and soft soap. On almost its first application, in the firemen's dispute, it has made union moderates look silly and union militants triumphant.

Then the bubble of complacency burst:

> On Wednesday, 12 December, there starts the rail go-slow; next day, Thursday, 13 December, November's trade figures are published; and the miners meet. This conjecture could conceivably lead the country on the twelfth day before Christmas into the worst national economic and social crisis since the war. (8 December 1973).

Yet the *Economist* continued to cling to the life-raft of the incomes policy:

> If stern steps have to be taken to stem a drain on sterling, it would be best to tackle cost inflation directly. This could be done by declaring another six months' freeze on wages and prices . . . no doubt giving a weekend's notice so that the miners, railwaymen and other combatant unions would have an incentive to hasten to settle before the freeze came . . .(15 December 1973)

The final debacle of the Heath Government was recorded without a sign of contrition, on 16 February 1974:

> In the past year rising import prices have moved the terms of trade 15 *per cent* against Britain, worsening the trade account by nearly £2 billion. Imported inflation put pressure on home costs and prices, cut into real incomes and made it necessary to offer generous wage limits for Stage three. The gamble was that world prices would fall and the unions would prove reasonable. Instead Britain has been highjacked into the double-figure inflation zone, by quadrupled oil prices and the miners' strike. (p.78).

And finally on 9 March 1974:

> The miners were bought off on Wednesday evening at a cost of about £103 million, double the offer first made to them and a rise of about 30 *per cent* in their wages.

The miracle had come to an end.

A Lone Voice of Dissent

All the items listed as characterizing British economic ideology are, I submit, contained in the above quotations: the promise of growth; the promise of a miracle; the certainty that these can be bought by expanding monetary demand; the faith in an incomes policy; the hectoring of those who disagree; the lecturing of other countries; and the ultimate disaster, from which eyes must be averted and for which alibis must be sought.

For purposes of comparison, and to show that this dissection of *The Economist* is based on something more than the privilege of hindsight, I conclude this section with a few quotations from a rival publication, *The Banker,* which took a very different view at the time. Thus it warned in the run-up to the March 1972 Budget that:

> Any further tax reliefs on the massive scale being talked of in the City would probably just make Britain's next boomlet quicker and less sustainable, and so damage rather than help industrial development.

When this advice was ignored, it concluded in May that:

> the Government appears committed to another attempt at breaking the fetters on Britain's economic growth by expanding demand . . . We would have preferred the Government to have given less away . . . and to have stuck a little more faithfully to its ideas for improving the long-term efficiency of the economy.

Thus there followed the floating of the pound:

> The shock decision was greeted with an extraordinary outburst of optimism which, in the opinion of *The Banker,* was inappropriate and short-sighted. To represent this forced, panic recognition of sterling's decline, and that of Britain as a stable economic power, as a victory for economic growth, a glorious defeat for the speculators, the opening of a new age of prosperity, that seems to us inexcusable.

Nor did *The Banker* share *The Economist's* complacency about the money supply. In September 1972 it wrote:

> A heavy price will have to be paid, in terms of prolonged price inflation, for allowing the country to be flooded with money in this abandoned and almost panic manner. The Bank of England should convince itself that the stability of the currency is at stake and tell the Government that it will now aim for a money supply growth rate of 10 to 12 *per cent* a year, whatever happens at those chats about incomes policies in Whitehall.

The Banker also achieved a better track record as soothsayer. Thus in April 1973, it forecast that:

> A radical new strategy for the UK economy will be required after the current dash for growth has run its course . . . There is considerable suspicion, to say the least, that a "stop" of uncertain magnitude will occur at a future date, but probably before year-end.

When nemesis duly arrived at the end of the year, *The Banker* was not inclined to let either the Government or its accomplices off lightly:

> Stop means stop; it does not mean go. The Government's growth gamble was bound to fail. Even without the "bad luck" of the continued rise in commodity prices the British economy could not have expanded fast enough to match the flood of demand created quite deliberately by the fiscal and monetary policies of the past two years . . . The current political slogans ("problems of success" etc.) cannot mask the truth — which is that one more dash for growth has ended . . . in a somersault. (December 1973).

> For Britain the past year has been a sad one, partly because of the Government's failure to understand the real opportunities that the Common Market presents, partly because of the eruption of social conflict at year-end, but mainly because of the lack of integrity of political and economic debate . . . When honourable newspapers, and leading economists, can so mislead and befuddle the people that, even on the brink of the precipice, most people were still saying that all was well and the country two-thirds of the way to an economic miracle (what will the other third be like?), then the governing classes of the country deserve no better than the crippling social conflict that they have become involved in. (January 1974).

5. The Role of Opinion Formers

WITHIN the triangle formed by economic research, governmental institutions and policy there exists a range of unofficial opinion-forming circles that concern themselves with evaluating current policy, intermediating the results of research in so far as they may be relevant to policy and keeping an eye on what is thought to be within the range of political acceptability. These groups maintain a rich variety of formal and informal links with the institutions and individuals charged with the conduct of policy. This is the area where policy choices are debated, alternative courses of action aired, and "practical" or "political" objections to some of them are registered. These groups may be seen as fulfilling a "filtering" function in so far as some policy options are ruled out at this stage. In some ways, the opinions current amongst these groups are more influential than those of the backbench MPs, the CBI, the TUC or the City.

This filtering function, the process by which policies become acceptable to informed opinion, is necessary for several reasons. First, policy variables are few, and the number of words and theories bearing upon them many: somehow all these ideas have to be focused on the only political question — *"que faire?"* Secondly, the people who have to carry out policy, or directly advise ministers, are themselves often members of these opinion groups, or they have a natural affinity with the members; their backgrounds are similar and they will be looking forward to a day when they can rejoin the groups free from the constraints of the Official Secrets Act; it is thus necessary to carry these people along with the policy choices being debated. Thirdly, these groups comprise the only people thought capable

61

of offering advice on the usually marginal changes in the policy instruments with which most economic debate in practice is about. Official advisers will therefore wish to keep their ears close to the ground, if only to avoid being caught unprepared by a question from a minister who has himself picked up some new idea from one of the groups.

As other observers have suggested, however, these opinion forming circles seem rather more incestuous in Britain than is healthy. There is a lack of really independent sources of analysis and advice about economic policy. Some stockbrokers have made noble efforts to fill the gap, but this is a very recent development. Banks have kept away from the limelight, though they are natural repositories of economic information and should have a natural interest in forecasting. Once upon a time, bank chairmen used to air their views about the state of the nation in their annual statements but after Keynes had made a few scathing remarks about such "twittering in the bushes" economic journalists kept teasing the banks until their chairmen more or less retired from the field. In contrast to American banks, the chairmen's oracular pronouncements have not, sadly, been replaced by modern economic analyses. There is the CBI, but that is a lobby for business.

The NIESR is subsidized by the government and its forecasting methods are similar to those used by the Treasury. This is not in itself wrong; but it is hardly a formula for lively public debates between opposing camps. Moreover, the NIESR's record shows that it has acted as an influence favouring expansionary policies; since it also has a history of high-level interchange of staff with the Treasury, its bias seems more likely to have accentuated that of the Treasury than offset it, in ghostly reflection of the stop-go economic cycle itself. None of the other teams has built up a long enough record to judge the quality of its advice; and some of them appear more interested in the theoretical implications of the data than employing a theoretical structure over a period of years to interpret events.

For whatever reason, there does not exist the atmosphere of lively cut-and-thrust amongst open-minded but informed analysts that is such a feature of the US scene. Nor is there anything equivalent to the German circle of economic advisers.

One cannot escape the impression, however unfair it may be, that many economists are more concerned with getting accepted on the inside track both politically (invitations to tea with the Chancellor etc.) and academically (where many of the chairs of economics and journals are occupied by fervent anti-monetarists). The arguments of those few who take a contrary view to that of the Establishment, such as the Institute of Economic Affairs, have until recently been ignored rather than answered.

Since economic research is expensive, the problem is partly a financial one — lack of market, outside government and outside of the universities. Such markets as do exist tend to be adequately catered for by economic journalists. In this field, there is the market for company chairmen who need to have opinions offered to them at which other company chairmen can nod gravely over the salmon; they want to be sure that the free market would work if it were allowed to but that there is no danger of them suddenly being catapulted into it. There is the market for middle managers who are not so sure free enterprise exists and is working; and that for academics and school teachers and Labour MPs who are pretty sure free enterprise has brought all our troubles upon us.

The economic journalists themselves are members of the opinion-forming groups. Like the economists, they are very interested in keeping up with what is "on" in terms of practical politics. However, all opinion-formers keep a weather eye on what is "off" too — like the incomes policy idea under Mr Heath's first few months in government — in case it suddenly becomes "on". It can become "on" either through "pressure of events" or through the opinion formers' own expression of their preferences. The well-known habit of journalists at functions given by ministers or other influential policy-makers, of arguing with each other rather than listening to their hosts is thus given an unexpected rationale.

But neither sophisticated forecasting nor influential journalism takes us to the heart of the opinion-forming circles. Pride of place must be given to the English tradition of informal, face-to-face, private discussions amongst top people. These are the groups to which would-be members of the establishment must attach themselves if they want to be accepted. The members include an elite corps of ex-opinion formers who have moved on to higher things: semi-official institutions, banking, industry, the European Commission, tribunals, royal commissions and pay boards, vice-chancellorships — they all claim their share. They all provide, in addition, further opportunities for formal and informal communication especially since the people involved have often known each other for a long time. The functions range from formal meetings to private dinner parties at which one "bumps into", maybe, Harold Lever, Labour's economic brain and link-man to the City; the quiet gathering at Brown's Hotel; the post-Budget inquisition of the Political Economy Club; the mumbled remark over lunch at the Reform.

Most of the traffic in messages is quite banal in content. Most of it consists of gossip, or talk about people — who's in and who's out. Nothing could be farther from the truth than the conspiracy theory of politics applied to UK economic policy. The way the Establishment works is not nearly systematic enough to deserve such a label. And a wide range of political views is tolerated. Even in private informal discussions the tradition of having as many "representative" views as possible is kept alive. Far less tolerance may be extended to those with fundamentally different economic ideas, especially when these challenge the professional assumptions of the key members of such groups. Yet they will be patiently listened to, also. The real function of these circles is to keep everybody up-to-date with what is "in", thus exerting subtle but insistent pressure towards conformity with the central, orthodox position. Which is all very fine so long as the central orthodox position is yielding successful policies; Keynes turned it upside down because it had failed; and now the tradition he started is itself on the defensive for having failed. The Establishment is again uneasy because it knows that one quick way into the Establishment is to be a successful rebel. (By "Establishment" I refer to the ethos espoused by the group of top civil servants, economists and journalists who feel, when they meet each other, that they are in the presence of another person who counts, who matters. Others exist, but do not matter. All credit to Henry Fairlie for the term).

This Establishment naturally treats official policy of the day with respect. The usual line is: past policies have been poor, but "now" the corner has been turned and policy is on the right lines. Since it is the opinions of these groups which are reflected in the policy, this attitude is not surprising. But an exaggerated respect is accorded to newly-elected governments, which therefore exploit it. Thus in the "Selsdon Man" period after the election in 1970, people who questioned whether it would work were informed that they would do well to receive the message: the new government would *not* help out ailing companies, a new philosophy of self-help *had* arrived, and the Prime Minister was *not* going to have cups of tea with TU leaders at 10 Downing Street. This rather upset the economic Establishment at the time — since most members are university "lib-lab" in their politics — but it adapted and passed the message on. These circles, including people from the City in them, were also touchingly keen to do what they could to help the Labour government during its National Plan phase in 1965-66, passing over the obvious absence of any strategy for dealing with the yawning balance of payments gap (surely the one aspect on which Keynesian economists were really qualified to give an opinion: yet those who tried to issue warnings were officially muzzled). Similarly in 1975-76 the message came through that it would be most useful if everybody could tell other countries please to reflate their economies, not just in Britain's interest, but in everybody's. That was after the collapse of the British boom of 1973, when the message had been that the press should, please, help to sustain the confidence: growth is largely a matter of learning to enjoy it. And the press did what it could.

Yet the messages are far from all one-way. Several individual journalists have made notable contributions to changing "acceptable" opinion in these opinion-forming groups, as have economists, on such matters as floating exchange rates, the proper margin of slack on which to run the economy, the way to reform the credit mechanism, taxation policy, policy with regard to overseas investment, devaluation (and especially policy after the 1967 devaluation), and regional policy.

So the Establishment is adaptable, efficient in spreading messages, but puts up long resistance to unorthodox ideas. It has helped to confine British economic debate to a regrettably

narrow range. It has assisted in the perpetuation of policies that had
plainly failed. It has, to say the least, not encouraged its members
to keep up with new developments in economic thought from
abroad. For those who wish to change fashion, it poses daunting
obstacles. But once fashion changes, everybody discovers that
that is what they really thought all along.

The Press

IT is easy for an economic journalist to exaggerate the influence
of the press. Most of the time, it is just a background presence.
Ministers read newspapers like the rest of us; so do their
advisers. As in other areas of policy, they probably do not
glean much hard economic information from the press that they
have not already received from other sources. They have to deal
with problems which never reach the newspapers at all. In
economic forecasting and comment the quality of the staff they
have at their command, and their access to other sources of
advice from academic economists and others (within the
conventions they work under), mean that the press generally
speaking will be some way behind events. Ministers are, however,
concerned with their press "image" and with getting their
policies across to informed opinion, and are often as sensitive
to criticism as an actor to a bad notice in the arts pages.

Ministers are prone to the feeling that the press is not really
doing as much as it might to be helpful in, for a current
instance, educating the people about the necessity of an incomes
policy. This is echoed in journalists' usual image of themselves,
as highly critical and independent if responsible observers of
affairs. My own impression – and here one has to lapse into the
use of the first person singular, a practice properly abhorred in
economic journalism – is that the press is usually, and in
general, supportive of and adaptive to official policy – all
official policy. Even with television, its main job after all is to
report news. And news, increasingly, is made by governments, or
is about economic developments – 30 *per cent* inflation, a run
on the pound – that only ministers can deal with. The reporting

function itself thus puts the spotlight on ministers – what they are expected to do, or what they are doing. Moreover, reporting is increasingly mixed with comment, open or implied.

Several forces interact here: (*a*) the journalist's professional interest in detecting signs of an impending change of policy as early as possible; (*b*) the government's control of news sources; (*c*) the government's interest in influencing comment – often the same as *(b)*; *(d)* the infinitely superior supporting staff of economists and so forth that official agencies have at their disposal; (*e*) the government's ability to determine the timing of news announcements – at least to some extent.

Working under severe time restraints, and in a highly complex area, journalists have to take a lot on trust. In covering such major events as Budget day, it is generally acknowledged that they do an excellent job, within the time available. But they have neither the time, nor the supporting staff, nor often the qualifications to question assumptions built into policy. In the normal course of events, their instinct would be to call up other sources of independent opinion, and report them. Yet as we have already seen, there are few of these independent sources in the field of macro-economic policy (excluding the obvious lobbies like the TUC or CBI or the "stockbroker in the City"). Official opinion and official sources command the field. The most authoritative outside source, the NIESR, has been biased in favour of growth policies; so that the comparison of the Chancellor's "Budget judgement" with that recommended by the NIESR will normally make the former appear unduly restrictive even if subsequent events show it to have been unduly expansionary. For the press, that is water under the bridge. By the time the next Budget comes around, there is a new reporting job to be done, a new official view, and a new NIESR view. True, this gap has been filled to some extent by the development of other forecasting units, but these have yet to make any big impact on the general thrust of news coverage.

Official sources usually use their powers over news and news sources with extreme care, and often with generosity. Normally, they become angry only in circumstances where anybody would, such as with journalists who break confidences – or what officials regard as confidences. Criticism as such is of course accepted, preferably if it can be balanced by other criticism so that the minister's action can be represented as being in the middle of the spectrum: "some said I did too much; others that I did too little; I'm happy" is a customary post-budget comment from a chancellor. If they do get cross with a particular journalist, however, that can cut off his raw material and the life-blood of his activity. It can happen.

The very task of having to bring out a newspaper every day imposes its own slant on news treatment. A paper cannot diverge all that far, nor for very long, from current measures of official policy because it will appear to be saying the same things day after day, (i.e. simply that government policy since a given date has been completely wrong so there is not much point in discussing the latest stupidity). However, its readers, it presumes, wish for report and comment on what is new that day. One solution, for a newspaper that decides that official policy is wrong, is to treat that day's news as if it were yet another proof of the need for a change. But this is too difficult to sustain for very long, unless it is thought that official policy will actually change in the desired direction: "Inflation is now running at 30 *per cent*; still the government dithers".

The patriotic gloss that ministers, especially prime ministers, often put on policies creates yet another problem for journalists. If a government in its wisdom decides that the over-riding national interest lies in a certain direction, then it is a courageous newspaper indeed which says that it does not. What is called a "decisive action" (that is, a "stop" following a sterling crisis) is usually presented in such patriotic or Dunkirk-spirit terms. Dunkirk was in fact a military debacle. But such an appeal is always treated favourably in the majority of newspapers. So is "going for growth".

The belief of many ministers that they have powers that King Canute lacked is not discouraged by such dramatization of "decisive action". Where economists of any school can often see how events build up over many months and years to produce some particular "headline catching" event on some particular day, politicians are encouraged by the press to think they can deal with that problem today and go on to tomorrow's problem after a sound night's sleep. "What would *you* have done in November 1973?", or "What would *you* have done in October 1976?" (both crisis months) fits this syndrome. The tendency towards short-term thinking is thus furthered by calls for action and by plaudits for action when it comes: "It is ridiculous to imagine that . . . cuts in public expenditure will have the slightest effect, even on the theory held by the monetarists, within the timescale within which it is essential for the country to produce results". Thus Mr Healey on his incomes policy in July 1975 (in answer to a question in the House of Commons put by Sir Geoffrey Howe): thus as always. The possibility that no course of action could achieve its effect within the sort of time-scale on which Whitehall habitually works is one which just does not occur to ministers or their officials.

Politicians, like journalists, cope with events as they happen. In that regard, they both speak the same language. Neither profession allows much time for reflection; neither predisposes its practioners to study the flow of events; both tend to exaggerate the role of personalities. Is Don Ryder the man to sort out the motor industry? How much can Jack Jones persuade the other TU leaders to swallow? Can Ronald Mackintosh get Neddy moving again? Can Denis Healey pull off his "delicate balancing act" before Phase III of the incomes policy? The fact is that the economy will be affected little by the personalities of these people compared with the effects exerted over quite a long time-scale by the macro-economic policy of the government. The sudden changes in opinion about who is a "good man" for any particular job and who is not should be sufficient warning that here we are dealing with symptoms, sometimes with scapegoats, not with causes. The press tends to encourage the confusion between the two. Looking back over the past 20 years, not even the personalities of individual chancellors have had any discernible impact on the *pattern* of macro-economic policy.

6. *The Vicious Circle*

IF policy has been driven on its erratic course by the conflict between two aims — to secure the strength of sterling, and to encourage economic growth — the debate between them has been between the deaf and dumb. Each side has come to regard its aim as good in its own right and, in the heat of the clash, the outward signs have come to be mistaken for the inner reality. Thus the Bank of England, backed by politicians on both sides of the House, has undoubtedly regarded a high exchange rate for the pound as a sign of healthy economy. Its main aim for 50 years has been to keep sterling's chin up. Going into the Bank, as journalists have to do, when there is a sterling crisis on, is like visiting a friend who has suffered a personal tragedy: if you are not weeping when you come out, you know you ought to be. Defeats are taken with stoic calm; forces are remarshalled: and the battle begins again.

On the other side are the "growth" doctors. They give priority to full employment, and they regard a high and rising level of demand as the sign of a healthy economy — because that encourages in their view not only full employment but also faster long-term economic growth. Their main frustration, at least until 1972, was the Bank of England's stout defence of "the virility symbol" of a particular sterling exchange rate. This was seen as holding the economy back from realizing its full potential. What should have been a partnership turned into a battle. The Bank knew that its strength lay in the regard with which the pound was held at home and abroad. Because it, at least initially, regarded the "growth" doctors as dangerous, since they would promote deficit financing and endanger the currency, it was led to exaggerate (even in its own mind) the importance of adhering to a particular parity of the pound, and came to regard a strong pound as synonymous with success not only in achieving a degree of economic stability but also in defeating the opposing forces. The "growth" school, on the other hand, knew that their strength lay in the absolute commitment of governments since 1944 to the objective of full employment. Growth, which started as a means to the achievement of full employment, gradually became an end in itself. Enlisting the name of Maynard Keynes, without his permission, in their cause, the expansionists came to regard the Bank's defence of sterling as the main obstacle to "growth", because it appeared to be putting external aims before domestic ones, and in their campaign were led gradually to exaggerate the benefits that would flow from "toppling" sterling.

Yet they could not and did not attack sterling or the Bank of England directly, any more than the Bank could say it was against full employment or growth. Instead, they ignored each other. Thus an unholy alliance — more like an unholy mess — was created whereby the Bank stuck to its symbol, and successfully persuaded governments to defend sterling, while expansionists got their way in the repeated dashes for growth by governments seeking re-election (1955, 1958, 1963, 1972).

The result of the Bank's effort to keep sterling's chin up was to render British exports uncompetitive in world markets; thus sacrificing entire export-orientated industries, such as the motor industry, and shouldering the country with massive overseas debts as almost every available asset or security was chucked into the defence of the pound. By contrast, the result of the "growth" school's occasional domination of policy at pre-election time was to build up a head of inflationary steam in the economy, which (with the support for sterling) burst through in the shape of external deficits and accelerating inflation after every election.

What was lost in this melée was the aim of domestic stability either for its own sake or as a precondition for a sustained upturn in investment. Worse, the qualifications and reservations of sensible members of each school were forgotten. Thus in 1967 those who advocated devaluation of the pound — though few ventured to do this at all in public — were clear that if taken at a time of "full employment" of labour and capital resources, the step had to be accompanied by a deflation to release resources for the balance of payments. By 1972, this had been forgotten. The ideology of "growth" had become that degree more vulgarized. The floating of the pound then was flanked by a 100 *per cent* increase in the money supply in 4 years and a public sector deficit widening to 10 *per cent* of GNP.

A knock-out blow was delivered by each party in this heavyweight contest. The real strength of the "growth" doctors was indeed their analysis of Britain's unbalanced and untenable *external* situation — both its excessive volume of short-term overseas liabilities and its grim balance of payments position resulting from failing competitiveness. But it was this area in which for sociological reasons they had to concede victory to the Bank (in the struggle for the soul of Government and the Treasury). The Bank's real strength, by contrast, lay in its view that deficit financing and "growth" financed by the printing press would lead to accelerating domestic inflation and no growth (though this was a conviction which was weakened by the increasing influence of Keynesian economics at the Bank). What came through into policy was the Bank's over-valuation of sterling and the growth school's inflation of domestic demand. Ironically, if either one or the other had been in sole command, British policy would at least have been more consistent.

In this way, theoretical economic positions, each of which is in itself intellectually respectable if taken in the round, turn into vulgar ideologies. These ideologies involve their proponents in inconsistencies, propaganda exercises and sometimes downright deceits that severely handicap economic debate. This is not a matter of personalities. One can indeed predict that if the executive directors of the Bank were set down in the NIESR office and told to produce a quarterly review, they would soon be advocating policies to maximize growth — an aim with which they have every sympathy — whilst the NIESR team, parachuted into Threadneedle Street, would soon be following sterling's every movement with apprehension and dismay. Yet if the implied external policy of the "growth" school — allowing

72

the pound to depreciate to the extent needed to offset the
differential between British and overseas inflation rates in the
past — and the internal policy of the Bank of England —
involving a return to price stability — had been followed all
these years, Britain might have trodden in the steps of its
successful continental competitors.

A Rich Store of Stupid Decisions

THE man British economists love to hate, Professor Harry
Johnson, has remarked that British economic policy since the
war has contained "a rich store of stupid decisions" (The
Times, 9 March 1976). Yet nobody in his right mind, including
I am sure Professor Johnson, would say that British policy
makers are more stupid than those of other countries. This
pamphlet has suggested that it is the institutional and social
environment within which they have worked which has tended
to make their policies "stupid".

A wide range of influences has been brought to bear on
policy-makers; and the policies they have adopted have had
wide-ranging results for the British economy and society. But
analysis must "zero in" on a narrow area — the policy-makers
themselves. It is not enough to explain their actions purely in
ad hoc terms — either as random responses to chance political
influences or as reflecting an acceptance of this-or-that economic
doctrine, whether it be "Keynesianism" or any other. Policy
has shown systematic biases, and has been subject to recurring
inconsistencies. The systematic and recurring features of policy
demand a systematic explanation.

The dominant strands in policy have been summarised on
page 48. The inconsistencies and biases in that ideology are
obvious. The following points attempt to draw some
conclusions: —

1. A belief in the efficacy of a sustained high pressure of
demand in the economy has gone along with a desire to keep
sterling strong or at least to prevent it from depreciating "too
much"; such a combination must result in an accumulation of

foreign indebtedness not for a short period but indefinitely. This is not possible. Yet the same people who have wanted a high pressure of demand have also been those often quick to alert public opinion to the disadvantages of a depreciation in sterling. Thus *The Economist* which, as already shown, led the demand for a boom in 1973 was later found to be warning on the dangers of a "sterling crisis" and then of the costs of devaluation when it came. On 27 March 1976 it told its readers: "Forget for the moment the boost to British exports following sterling's plunge. How large are the capital losses which the government, other public sector bodies and major British companies have suffered on their foreign currency borrowings?" (Its answer was in a table showing the exchange cost to the taxpayer on public sector borrowing alone of £865.5 millions). This may have been entertaining journalism; the newspaper was, however, in effect complaining about the results of the expansionary policies it had consistently recommended. Yet even without such internal inconsistencies, the relationships between the institutions that influenced policy — notably the deference shown to each other by the Bank of England and the City on one hand and the growth doctors on the other — were likely to produce the same results.

2. During the restrictive phases of policy, there has often been a disire to keep aggregate monetary demand under control, but this control has gone along with a desire to keep interest rates low (at any given exchange rate). The natural ally of those who wish to keep demand under restraint has been the Bank of England — the institution which has also been most unwilling to let interest rates go as high as would be required to fund the government's borrowing needs without adding to the money supply. Again, these two desires are not possible to satisfy simultaneously, in logic or practice.

3. Since both schools have been rent by internal contradictions the institutions concerned have readily linked up in agreeing that the solution lies outside market economics altogether — in physical controls, incomes policies and planning. Even if such policies have arguments in their favour, which is debatable, the failure to resolve the contradictions in the institutions making policy at the overall "macro" level meant that these other policies were likely to be tried in conditions least conducive to

their success — with the general level of demand in the economy and the balance of payments driven this way and that by fluctuating monetary and fiscal conditions.

4. The maximum level of unemployment deemed to be politically acceptable has itself fluctuated considerably over time — from Beveridge's 8 *per cent* to 1.5 *per cent* in the 1950s and back to 4 *per cent* or so today. The only consistent feature has been that at any one time the level thought likely to accompany measures to combat inflation through demand restraint has been believed to be "too high". The people who have been most insistent on this have not been the politicians but economists — i.e. people neither elected nor qualified to give political judgements but people whose opinions about economic policy are important in sustaining or undermining a politician's confidence in his policies.

5. On some issues Keynesians and monetarists have come together to prevent full study being given to policy options when these have seemed to fly in the face of the conventional interpretations of both doctorines. For instance, the possibility of improving the trade-off in the long term between unemployment and inflation — so that less inflation and lower long-term unemployment could be achieved simultaneously — by a government showing itself determined to stop inflation even at the high cost of high, temporary, unemployment has not been fully investigated despite the evidence that this is the policy adopted by some other countries such as Germany. Keynesians have rejected it because they believe that governments can stimulate (rather then restrict) demand to achieve full employment, and should do so, and monetarists because they do not believe there is a "trade-off" in the long term (i.e. the long-term rate of unemployment is fixed by factors not susceptible to macro-economic policy).

6. Until very recently, sterling tended to be supported in the short term at levels that were invariably shown to be unsustainable in the longer term (leading to an unneccesary loss of reserves and accumulation of debts) because of such factors as the role played by the Bank of England in influencing policy and the (mostly mistaken) belief that the City of London wanted sterling to be supported (to maintain a pre-determined exchange rate). Then when, in early 1976, the Bank and the

Treasury agreed for once that the rate for the pound was too *high*, so unaccustomed were the thought processes involved that the market was handled with staggering ineptitude.

7. The international role of the City of London has influenced policy in three respects. First, its international skills and credit have enabled governments to borrow funds from abroad to help finance deficits in the balance of payments or the Budget, postponing adjustments in domestic policy which governments were always going to be forced to make — usually in less propitious circumstances — in the end. Secondly, the habits of an international reserve currency centre — running up overseas liabilities with impunity — lived on after the conditions which once had made it possible for Britain to conduct such a policy had passed away. In the old days, these liabilities were unlikely to be drawn down by their holders (for whom they were assets to be held in London for their own convenience indefinitely) but now they are all too likely to be drawn down — having to be repaid out of future UK payments surpluses. Thirdly, the City has looked for its major expansion overseas and has not placed the pressure it might otherwise have done on the government to follow "sound money" domestic policies. For all these reaons, the City of London, far from providing a bulwark against inflation, has been an efficient piston in the engine of deficit finance.

8. Policy has repeatedly failed to achieve any of its aims, not because of an inherent fault in the two-party system or an inherently destabilizing conflict between the "logic of democracy" and the "logic of the market economy" (plenty of other countries maintain the two in reasonable equilibrium) but because of identifiable faults in the institutions and ideologies that have shaped policy.

7. *Planning the Escape*

THE advent of North Sea oil presents a marvellous opportunity for Britain to release itself from the economic prison to which it has been confined for far too long. Unless the pattern of economic policy changes, however, this opportunity will be wasted. Demand will again be stimulated excessively. The real resources gained by the exploitation of the country's mineral resources will be diverted into consumption, not investment. Inflation will again accelerate. The balance of payments, after a short-lived recovery, will again dive into the red. There is little sign on the existing economic or political scene of any element strong enough to force a change of policy that would make future business cycles essentially different from those of the "go-stop" past.

The temptations to politicians to follow economic policies that would dissipate the opportunity are considerable. To stimulate demand would keep consumption up (especially consumption of imports) — for a time. It might keep their party in office — for a time. All the old economic arguments would again be employed in defence of such a policy — above all, the argument that it was the way to get "growth" going.

Those who wish to change policy have two ways of proceeding. One is to appeal to "the truth" — to try to convince those who hold conventional views that they are logically wrong, to try to argue the case rationally, either from first principles or by an appeal to the evidence. This is the method of science, taken over into the area of economic behaviour. The other approach is to lay bare the reasons why people should continue to hold certain opinions even when the case against them is strong. The former approach is more respectable, because it is supposed to be more polite and scientific ("play the ball, not the man"). But this is not so. For the last resort of those who take this line is to accuse their opponents of sheer stupidity. The latter approach, by contrast, ends by accusing them only of acting out of self-interest or self-deception. The ideal approach is to use the second method, whilst persuading "scientific" opinion that one is only using the first. That is how Keynes founded the institutions of neo-Keynesianism: using all the polemical weapons at his disposal to discredit conventional thinking whilst gaining academic disciples as well.

Britain's inflation is the product of the institutions of neo-Keynesianism. Within these institutions, the acceptable range of economic opinion has been restricted. The costs to an individual of changing his beliefs have thus been raised. Job opportunities for those taking opposing views have been few; the levers of power offered only to those within the fold. Economic crises have been treated as reasons for creating further levers of control (for neo-Keynesians to manipulate), rather than as reasons for changing beliefs. Given the absence of strong independent sources of opinion, either within the universities or without, and given the close inter-connection between academic economists and the establishment, every adverse turn in Britain's economic fortunes has been used to reinforce conventional opinions. Increasingly, those who insist on taking unconventional views have been obliged to emigrate. Increasingly, the country has lost the means whereby it can be kept in touch with overseas opinion. Where is the banker in Britain who can speak up on behalf of the market system as Walter Wriston, Chairman of Citibank, regularly does in the United States? Where is the British university capable now of producing a Friedman, or a Hayek or even a Jacques Rueff?

Instead, countries which are in fact following successful policies, like Germany and the United States, are treated to the scorn of the British establishment, of British newspapers and British Chancellors of the Exchequer. Thus in the aftermath of the oil-price increase, Britain of course expanded domestic demand, when every other country but Sweden said the crisis required a once-and-for-all process of adjustment. It is these latter countries, which got their adjustment over quickly, that have been able since then to bring down unemployment. But there was nobody in Britain to contradict establishment opinion in 1974. Outside the ranks of a few notable economic journalists (Samuel Brittan, Peter Jay, Patrick Hutber) where were the voices of dissent in Britain in 1974? As silent as they had been at the beginning of the Tory boom in 1972.

It is possible that those on the Left and Right who regard Britain's inflation as being the product of deep-seated social problems are correct. Anything is possible. Maybe the public school system, withdrawal from Empire, Trade Union pressure or class conflict did have something to do with it. This study argues that such explanations are not necessary. It is not necessary for a "big" phenomenon (such as British inflation) to have a "big" cause. The explanation may be something more mundane, and the remedy may lie in the hands of an élite, not in deep sociological factors beyond the reach of therapy.

Institutions, once established, are not easily dislodged, because they embody interests as well as ideas. The immediate aftermath of a major war is invariably a fertile breeding-ground for new institutions. Germany was fortunate in emerging from World War II with a group of economists (such as Eucken and Muller-Armack) ready to supply an economic doctrine that relied on the market mechanism rather than dirigisme. The experience of living under a dictatorship (and doubtless American influence too) was just as influential as the memory of the inflation of 1923 in gaining initial acceptance for this doctrine. It found a champion in Erhard. It caused unemployment, initially, but then it began to produce results. The doctrine of reasonably balanced budgets and reliance on markets, and an independent central bank, became institutionalized. In Britain, by contrast, it was precisely in this period that neo-Keynesianism became institutionalized.

Politicians everywhere want quick results and snatch at "controls". But only in Britain is there such an absence of countervailing influences, whether from academics, independent research organisations, the financial community or (some might add) from the Church. Instead, the country's top economists spend their time egging on the politicians to push this lever or pull that, or better still invent brand new levers which only they, the economists, know how to use. These people have no human understanding of business men, and no idea of entering into a genuine partnership with them. They manipulate their subjects with all the arrogance of an eighteenth century aristocrat handling his labourers, but without his sympathy.

Max Weber attributed the rise of capitalism partly at least to the working out in practical life of a belief in the "Protestant ethic". He was not concerned with the question of whether Protestantism was "true" or not, but with the practical effects of the motives it supplied for hard work and frugality. In a similar way, the practical effects of the acceptance by governments and economists of a belief in the Keynesian paradigm can be traced in terms of the typical pattern of policy actions to which it gives rise. This typical pattern of policy actions includes in particular the ready manipulation of aggregate demand in the economy (in the interests of "fine tuning"), the downgrading of monetary influences on economic behaviour and a willingness to resort to controls rather than the market mechanism. In the absence of countervailing influences, it also pre-disposes policy makers towards a very short-term view of policy actions. If, for instance, unemployment is seen as the product of a policy rather that of the structure of society or the behaviour of economic units, obviously policy can and should be directed to eliminating unemployment forthwith. The older paradigm, which neo-Keynesianism replaced, stressed the virtues of reasonable monetary stability and balanced budgets on the implicit assumption that these were the chief contributions that government could make to the economy, in that they alone provided individuals with a firm framework in which to make their own plans and live their own lives. Economic growth was a by-product of such an environment. It was the private commercial banking system, not the government, that created the "aggregate demand" necessary to fuel the industrial revolution in Britain. What is significant is that many of the world's most successful economies in the past 20 years have adhered to this older paradigm as a guide to policy (whilst dressing it sometimes in Keynesian "national income" clothes). Not only Germany, but also countries as diverse as France, the United States, the Scandinavian countries, Brazil, Hong Kong, Switzerland, Malaysia and Singapore have followed essentially conservative and prudent financial policies. However, these countries adopted varied policies with regard to other aims (such as welfare policies).

There is no reason for liberals or even socialists to be frightened of "sound-money". They can pursue their political aims, whether these be re-distribution of wealth or a low level of expenditure on defence, within a framework of financial stability and a mixed economy. In these countries, most of the big political parties work within such a framework. In Britain, none of the political parties has done so. The institutions of neo-Keynesianism have been too strong and the voice of common sense, though it has guided Britain through a thousand years of history, too weak.

8. Sources

The United Kingdom in 1980: The Hudson Report.
(Associated Business Programmes Ltd, 1974).

Economic Growth in Modern Britain, Anthony Peaker,
Macmillan Studies in Economics, (MacMillan 1974).

Price and Investment Relationships, Sir Robert Shone,
(Elek, 1975).

Britain's Economic Prospects, Richard Caves and Associates,
(George Allen and Unwin, 1968).

Economic Change in England, 1880 – 1939, R.S. Sayers
(Oxford Paperback University Series, 1967).

Forecasting the UK Economy, J.C.K. Ash and D.J. Smyth,
(Saxon House Studies, 1974).

The Stagnant Society, Michael Shanks,
(Penguin Special, 1961).

British Economic Policy Since the War, Andrew Shonfield,
(Penguin Books Ltd., 1958 [revised 1959]).

Steering the Economy, Samuel Brittan,
being an extensively revised and enlarged edition of **The Treasury
under the Tories,**1964, 1969, 1971.

Second Thoughts on Full Employment Policy, Samuel Brittan,
(Barry Rose for Centre for Policy Studies, 1975).

Monetary Policy for Stable Growth, E. Victor Morgan,
Hobart Paper 27, (Institute of Economic Affairs, 1964).

The Growth of the Economy,
(National Economic Development Council, 1964).

What Attitude to Growth? David Lomax,
National Westminster Bank Quarterly Review, February 1974.

Money in Boom and Slump, Alan Walters,
Hobart Paper 44, (Institute of Economic Affairs, 1969.
Second edition, 1970).

Economic Growth in Western Europe 1870 – 1959, Angus
Maddison, (Banca Nazionale del Lavoro Quarterly Review,
March 1959).

The Economist, leading articles 1960 – 1976, passim.

**National Institute of Economic and Social Research Quarterly
Reviews,** passim.

Economic Growth in Britain, ed. P.D. Henderson,
(Weidenfeld and Nicholson, 1966).

How Much Unemployment? John Wood,
IEA Research Monograph 28, 1970. IEA Occasional Paper 44,
1975, Milton Friedman.

British Economic Policy 1970 – 1974: Two Views,
Ralph Harris and Brendon Sewill, Hobart Paperback No. 7.